Misled

Is God Calling His People to Leave the Roman Catholic Church?

Kenneth March

Dedication

This book is dedicated to the one billion plus Catholics around the world who have been misled and disillusioned by the Roman Catholic Church.

God wants a personal relationship with each of them. Instead they were led into an empty relationship with an institution that taught them many things that are in error...things that are in conflict with God's Word as found in the Holy Bible.

Preface

A Note to Catholics and Former Catholics
from Ken March

This book was written for Catholics and former Catholics around the world who have been misled and disillusioned by the Catholic Church. You were taught many things as spiritual truths that are in direct conflict with God's Word as found in the Holy Bible.

You have heard things that have made you want to distance yourself from the Church. Thousands of priests sexually molesting, raping and sodomizing innocent children who were entrusted into their spiritual care. Church leaders keeping these horrific violations out of the eye of the public through an elaborate culture of secrecy, deception, and intimidation, and moving guilty priests from one parish to another. Then there are the frequent rumors of rampant homosexuality, financial scandals and intrigue at the highest levels of the Church.

Whether you are one of the devout faithful or have stopped going to mass but continue to call yourself a Catholic, it is my hope that this book will help you move away from a relationship with the organization known as *The Roman Catholic Church* and into a personal relationship with the living God who reveals himself to us in the Bible.

I have sought to support everything presented in this book with quotations from Scripture. Some things you read may force you to reevaluate beliefs you have held, or at least ones you have accepted as being true…perhaps taught to you by well-meaning parents, nuns or priests. That will be a good thing; it's important to always check our beliefs against God's Word.

Unless stated otherwise, all scripture verses are from the New Living Translation of the Bible (NLT). I have used the NLT for it's easy to understand English, but you don't have to. Get out your own Bible…whatever translation you have…and look up any verses you question.

Catholic and Protestant Bibles are pretty much the same and contain the same truths, except that Catholic Bibles include seven additional books known as Apocryphal books that are not in Protestant Bibles. Those books are Tobias, Judith, 1 Maccabees, 2 Maccabees, the Wisdom of Solomon, Sirach and Baruch. They can be found interspersed with other Old Testament books. In the section on Purgatory (Chapter 3), there is an explanation of why Protestants do not accept these books as being inspired by God.

This book deals with matters of eternal importance, so please do not blindly accept anything that I or anyone else tells you to be the truth. You must make informed decisions for yourself.

KennethMarch@rocketmail.com

Contents

Chapter 1

Scripturally Unsupported Teachings of Protestant and Catholic Churches

Ask a Catholic, "Are you a Christian?" and the common response will be, "No, I'm Catholic."

Actually the basic tenets of the Catholic Church and most mainstream Christian Protestant faiths are the same. They profess that God sent his one and only Son, Jesus, to be born of a virgin (Mary), to live a sinless life, and to suffer and die for the sins of the world. God did this to reveal himself and his love for mankind. He did it because sinful man could never measure up to his standard of holiness, and only God's sinless Son could pay the full price for mankind's sins. As a result, eternal life is ours if we trust that what Jesus did for us was full payment for our sins, and invite him to be the Lord of our lives. So you can be both a Catholic and a Christian if you believe these things.

Unfortunately, as with any church body that has been around for a long time, and the Catholic Church has been around the longest, certain beliefs inevitably creep in that are not supported by Biblical Scripture. Once a particular belief has been voted on and accepted as truth by a church body, it becomes a doctrine of that church, and nothing short of the physical appearance of God himself in all his glory will convince anyone to re-open the matter for further discussion.

As the centuries pass these non-Biblical doctrines accumulate and take the church farther and farther from the truth of God's Word. Such is the case with the Catholic Church.

Nearly every person reading this book will find something that calls into question one or more of their long-held beliefs. I urge the reader to do his or her best to keep an open mind. Many if not most of the beliefs we hold, or have held, came to us by way of other human beings, and many are not supported by Holy Scripture. If you believe, as I do, that the Holy Bible is the inspired Word of God, then we must base our beliefs solely on the Word and not on human conceived doctrines or interpretations that are not clearly supported by Scripture. We must always ask ourselves, *"Does what I believe in this area come solely from God's Word, or did it come from man?"* If it comes from man, it should be suspect, and recognized as non-essential to the Christian faith.

Those with considerable theological training may be the most challenged by some of the things presented in this book. They may have had scholarly professors, whom they greatly respected, who taught them things they accepted as truth without personally confirming that they were supported by Scripture. That is not to suggest that each and every one of *my* theological conclusions is correct. Holy Spirit filled believers can differ in their interpretations. No one has a monopoly on the exegesis of God's Word.

Unless noted, I have used the New Living Translation (NLT) when quoting Scripture because it is so easy to understand.

Unsupported Protestant Church Doctrines

Protestant denominations are not exempt from the accumulation of beliefs that are not supported by Scripture.

Unfortunately, many people think of the various protestant denominations as different "religions." Nothing could be farther from the truth. Most major protestant denominations (Methodist, Lutheran, Presbyterian, Pentecostal, Baptist, Seventh Day Adventist, etc.) profess the same basic Christian beliefs as the Catholic Church. They are Christian churches, and the religion is Christianity.

In most cases the various denominations have separated themselves from one another due to relatively minor doctrinal differences. Instead of demonstrating the kind of unity that Jesus prayed for in John 17, they have demonstrated the opposite…a disappointing disunity that has confused much of the world about the essential message of Christianity.

> *I* (Jesus) *am praying not only for these disciples but also for all who will ever believe in me through their message. I pray that they will all be one, just as you and I are one – as you are in me, Father, and I am in you. And may they be in us* <u>*so that the world will believe you sent me*</u>*. I have given them the glory you gave me, so they may be one as we are one. I am in them and you are in me.* <u>*May they experience such perfect unity that the world will know that you sent me and that you love them as much as you love me*</u>*. – John 17:20-23*

It seems to me that the peculiar areas of doctrinal differences that each denomination has that set them apart from all of the other mainstream protestant denominations may be their weakest areas of theology. Here are a few examples:

Missouri Synod Lutherans zealously insist that the bread and wine in Holy Communion are the *true* body and blood of Jesus, and will not tolerate the suggestion that they may *represent* the body and blood. They say the actual body and blood of Jesus is "in, with and under" the bread and wine, a somewhat nebulous concept that is as difficult to articulate as it is to substantiate.

Seventh Day Adventists insist that Saturday is the true Sabbath day, not Sunday. They may be technically correct. In addition they do not celebrate Easter or Christmas and look down on any member who is not a vegetarian.

Some Baptists believe drinking, dancing, wearing makeup and playing cards are sinful, un-Godly activities.

Pentecostals emphasize the importance of the gift of speaking in tongues to the extent that anyone who does not speak in tongues may be suspected of not really having the Holy Spirit in them.

And so it goes, one group of Christians judging another group of Christians based on secondary criteria that are non-essential to salvation.

Satan is so crafty! He understands the principle of "divide and conquer." And boy has he been successful in dividing God's church on earth, often based on inconsequential differences. God's message of salvation has been incoherent to much of the world because of this petty bickering between denominations. Instead of recognizing their brethren as being fellow members of the Body of Christ, some will not even fellowship with believers of another denomination; perhaps they fear their "pure" doctrine will somehow become polluted by association.

Some denominations would not even have allowed the recently deceased and revered Reverend Dr. Billy Graham to speak in their church because he did not subscribe to all of their idiosyncratic beliefs. How patient our Lord is to put up with such childish nonsense from those he loves!

It seems to me that there may currently be a movement by the Holy Spirit throughout the world that is beginning to bring various Christian denominations together. What a powerful testimony it would be to the love of God if they all began to work together to communicate the message of salvation through Jesus Christ to the world.

Unsupported Catholic Church Doctrines

As already mentioned the Catholic Church's core principals of salvation by grace alone through faith in the redemptive sacrifice of Jesus Christ remains intact; however, the number and magnitude of non-Biblical doctrines that have accumulated over the centuries have rendered the Catholic Church almost unrecognizable as a Bible believing Christian church body.

Mary, the Mother of Jesus, was Without Sin

The Catholic Church's doctrine of the Immaculate Conception was first pronounced by the church in 1854. This doctrine says that Mary was conceived without original sin. In other words, she was sinless her whole life. It seems this idea was not even a tradition of the early church until around 1100 AD, and it has no Scriptural support.

Mary Remained a Virgin for Life

This is another Catholic Church doctrine that is hard to defend.

> *Then they scoffed, "He's just the carpenter's son, and we know Mary, his mother, and his brothers—James, Joseph,[a] Simon, and Judas. 56 All his sisters live right here among us. Where did he learn all these things?" – Matthew 13:55-56*

Believers Should Pray to Saints

The Council of Trent, held in three parts from 1545 to 1563, first clarified the Catholic Church's doctrine that saints in heaven pray for those who are living, thus believers are told that their prayers have greater value if they are presented to God by Mary or other saints interceding on their behalf. The Bible never says that saints (believers in Jesus Christ who have preceded us in death) pray for us, or for that matter, that they can even see or hear us.

The Assumption of Mary

In 1950 Pope Pius XII announced as Catholic Church doctrine that at the end of Mary's life here on earth, she was taken body and soul into heaven. It was not stated as to whether she was taken alive or dead. Most Catholic theologians presume that she died first.

The Pope is the Vicar of Christ

The claim is that the Pope is God's appointed head over the Christian church on earth, and that when he speaks as Christ's vicar, he is infallible and all Christians must obey him. A few words of Jesus have been embellished and expanded to support this doctrine of the Church.

Purgatory

Declared by the Catholic Church to be a place of temporary punishment where the deceased goes to pay for minor, pardonable, but unrepented sins so they will be qualified to enter the heaven of a holy God. This teaching comes primarily from one of the books of the Apocrypha which are not recognized as being the inspired Word of God by non-Catholic believers.

We will discuss these and other doctrines of the Roman Catholic Church in more depth a little later.

Chapter 2

If Protestant and Catholic Church Doctrines are Imperfect, Why Focus on Catholic Church Shortcomings?

Satan is at work in all of our churches, both Catholic and Protestant. We have already discussed how he has been able to confuse much of the world into thinking that the various Christian denominations are different religions, making people wonder which, if any of them, is right.

Why then is this book focused primarily on unscriptural Catholic Church doctrines? First and foremost, it is because many Catholic doctrines serve to turn the parishioner's attention away from Jesus Christ, the glorious head of the church on earth! <u>Anyone or anything that redirects our praise, honor, worship or prayers from God to anyone or anything else is in grave error and is sinning against God.</u>

Jesus is the King of Kings, the Lord or Lords, the Lamb of God, the Light of the World and the one and only Son God. His name is above every name, and he has been given all power in heaven and on earth.

> *For a child is born to us, a son is given to us. The*
> *government will rest on his shoulders. And he will be*

called: Wonderful Counselor, Mighty God, Everlasting Father, Prince of Peace. – Isaiah 9:6

Looking for Jesus in Saint Peter's

I had the opportunity of touring Saint Peter's Basilica in Vatican City, the largest church building in the world. It is a truly magnificent, architectural wonder of approximately 240,000 square feet containing 44 altars, 11 domes and 778 columns. For a perspective, the average Walmart Supercenter is about 179,000 square feet, and nowhere near as tall. One dome rises to 448 feet from the floor.

There is gorgeous imported marble of many colors from all over the world, priceless tapestries, gold, silver and precious jewels. From a strictly monetary standpoint, it is thought it would cost many billions of dollars if one were to try to replicate St. Peter's, not including the many priceless works of art by renowned masters. One such piece is Michelangelo's Pieta, a beautiful work of art in white marble depicting the lifeless body of our Lord cradled in the arms of his mother, Mary.

The Pieta

One might think that if this is how a 17th century pope is honored in St. Peter's Basilica, the memorials to Jesus Christ must be so much more fabulous.

As I wandered through this massive cathedral with 395 statues honoring pope's, kings and saints, it struck me that for all of the opulence and magnificence there was virtually nothing glorifying the King of Kings and Lord of Lords! There were many images of baby Jesus in the arms of Mary, and small images of Jesus on the cross, but I saw only one large statue of Jesus. He is seated, surrounded by statues of Moses, Elijah and a pope. As I stood there I thought, "The Son of God couldn't even get a nice big statue of his own. He has to share the space with a bunch of dead guys." Oops! I meant to think, "deceased saints."

In addition I saw one statue of Jesus on the exterior colonnade. If you look carefully, you can spot him in the below photo on top of the building, second from the left, holding a cross. He is among 139 other statues of deceased saints.

I have a hard time expressing the profound disappointment and resentment I felt as I left this magnificent edifice in which no attempt was made to give Jesus Christ, the Savior of the World, the honor and glory he is entitled to.

> *Therefore, God elevated him to the place of highest honor and gave him the name above all other names, [10] that at the name of Jesus every knee should bow, in heaven and on earth and under the earth, [11] and every tongue declare that Jesus Christ is Lord, to the glory of God the Father.– Philippians 2:9-11*

By way of comparison, below is a photo of the 125 foot tall statue *Christ the Redeemer* towering over the City of Rio de Janeiro in Brazil. The money to build it came from Brazil's Catholic community. Well done!

Christ is the visible image of the invisible God. He existed before anything was created and is supreme over all creation, [16] for through him God created everything in the heavenly realms and on earth. He made the things we can see and the things we can't see—such as thrones, kingdoms, rulers, and authorities in the unseen world. Everything was created through him and for him. [17] He existed before anything else, and

he holds all creation together.[18] Christ is also the head of the church, which is his body. - Colossians 1:15-18

The Veneration of Mary

An Altar to Mary

We have an enemy who seeks our destruction. He is very real and incredibly cunning and deceitful. Satan works day and night to keep people from the intimate and exclusive relationship that God wants to have with them. I think he saw in Mary someone of whom no one could speak evil and he seized the opportunity. The Bible warns us about him.

> *Stay alert! Watch out for your great enemy, the devil.*
> *He prowls around like a roaring lion, looking for*
> *someone to devour. – 1 Peter 5:8*

The thief's (Satan's) *purpose is to steal and kill and destroy. My* (Jesus') *purpose is to give them a rich and satisfying life. - John 10:10*

Mary was chosen by God himself to be the earthly mother of the Savior of the World. The angel Gabriel called her blessed, and so she was, chosen to bear and help raise the Son of God who set aside his deity in order to take on human form.

> *"Don't be afraid, Mary, for you have found favor with*
> *God! You will conceive and give birth to a son, and you*
> *will name him Jesus. He will be very great and will be*
> *called the Son of the Most High...his Kingdom will*
> *never end!" – Luke 1:30-33*

I like something I once heard...that God probably chose Mary for that greatest of honors because, "she was willing." How many teenage girls would be willing to unjustly endure the gossip, the sneers and the condemnation of her family, friends and neighbors? Mary was even willing to face the death penalty in a society that was not at all accepting of an unmarried, pregnant teenager. To her everlasting credit, Mary's response to the angel was...

> *"I am the Lord's servant. May everything you have said*
> *about me come true." – Luke 1:38*

Mary must have also had other wonderful personal qualities that made her God's choice for raising his one and only Son. But let's be clear. Mary is <u>not</u> the mother of God! God has existed from eternity; Mary was a human being. In a verse prophesying the birth of Jesus, we read...

But you, O Bethlehem Ephrathah, are only a small village among all the people of Judah. Yet a ruler of Israel, <u>whose origins are in the distant past</u>, will come from you on my behalf. – Micah 5:2

Even Jesus was faced with people who wanted to venerate his mother. He redirected a woman's attention to where it should be, to God.

> *As he was speaking, a woman in the crowd called out, "God bless your mother—the womb from which you came, and the breasts that nursed you!"* [28] *Jesus replied, "But even more blessed are all who hear the word of God and put it into practice." – Luke 11:27-28*

To be sure, I am not saying anything negative about Mary. We all know how protective sons can be of their mothers, and I certainly would never want to get on Jesus' bad side (so to speak).

Another altar to Mary

19

The Veneration of Saints

The Bible uses the term "saint" to refer to any person who has accepted Jesus as their Lord and Savior and is therefore on their way to heaven, or one who has already arrived there.

The Catholic Church means something altogether different when it speaks of "saints." It uses the term to mean those persons whom it has designated as "saints." There are strict criteria for sainthood as established by the Catholic Church. One of these criteria is that the person has performed three verifiable miracles. Let me stop right there!

I believe that every verifiable miracle has been done solely by the power of God, and usually by invoking the name of Jesus Christ. I and countless other Christians have laid hands on the sick, praying in the name of Jesus, and witnessed miraculous healings, but I have never healed anyone! Nor do I believe has any other human being.

In the Book of Acts, chapter 3, we read about a miracle involving St. Peter. People immediately presumed that Peter had performed the miracle, but a short while later he explains that it was not him who did it, but God.

> *Peter said, "I don't have any silver or gold for you. But I'll give you what I have. <u>In the name of Jesus Christ the Nazarene, get up and walk!</u>" Then Peter took the lame man by the right hand and helped him up. And as he did, the man's feet and ankles were instantly healed and strengthened. He jumped up, stood on his feet, and*

> *began to walk! Then walking, leaping, and praising*
> *God, he went into the Temple with them. – Acts 3:6-8*

In Peter's words you can hear his total confidence that God was willing to, and would, heal in the name of Jesus. It was God who did the healing, not Peter. Peter says so...

> *All the people saw him walking and heard him praising*
> *God. [10] When they realized he was the lame beggar they*
> *had seen so often at the Beautiful Gate, they were*
> *absolutely astounded! [11] They all rushed out in*
> *amazement to Solomon's Colonnade, where the man*
> *was holding tightly to Peter and John. [12] Peter saw his*
> *opportunity and addressed the crowd. "People of*
> *Israel," he said, "what is so surprising about this? <u>And</u>*
> *<u>why stare at us as though we had made this man walk</u>*
> *<u>by our own power or godliness? [13] For it is the God of</u>*
> *<u>Abraham, Isaac, and Jacob—the God of all our</u>*
> *<u>ancestors—who has brought glory to his servant Jesus</u>*
> *<u>by doing this</u>. - Acts 3:9-8*

God does miracles. People do not, and that includes people the Catholic Church has designated as "saints."

We can call the Paul of the Bible Saint Paul because he fought the good fight and went to be with our Lord, trusting in the salvation that Jesus won for him by his death on the cross. Not because the Catholic Church officially decreed him to be a "saint."

As mentioned earlier, Catholic Church doctrine holds that saints in heaven pray for those who are living, and believers are told that their prayers have greater value if they are presented to God by Mary or other saints interceding on their behalf.

I would like to have been a fly on the wall the first time the suggestion was made that people should pray to dead saints! I wonder what kind of reaction that proposal initially garnered.

There is nothing in the Bible that tells us that people who have died can see or hear anything that goes on here on earth. There is most certainly nothing to suggest that we should pray to them and many Scriptures that make it clear we should not.

There is no gentle way to say this...a church that turns hearts and minds from God toward anyone or anything besides God is advocating ***idol worship***. This is a flagrant violation of the first commandment.

> *"You must not have any other god but me. ⁴ You must not make for yourself <u>an idol of any kind or an image of anything in the heavens or on the earth or in the sea.</u> ⁵ <u>You must not bow down to them or worship them</u>, for I, the LORD your God, am a jealous God who will not tolerate your affection for any other gods." – Exodus 20:3-5*

God tells us many times in Scripture that he is a jealous God.

> *"But be very careful! You did not see the LORD's form
> on the day he spoke to you from the heart of the fire at
> Mount Sinai. ¹⁶ So do not corrupt yourselves by making
> an idol in any form—whether of a man or a woman,
> ¹⁷ an animal on the ground, a bird in the sky, ¹⁸ a small*

> *animal that scurries along the ground, or a fish in the*
> *deepest sea. [19] And when you look up into the sky and*
> *see the sun, moon, and stars—all the forces of heaven—*
> *don't be seduced into worshiping them. The* LORD *your*
> *God gave them to all the peoples of the earth. –*
> *Deuteronomy 4:15-19*

Despite God's many warnings, the practice of idol worship by the Israelites resulted in the destruction of the nation and the dispersion of the Jewish people to many nations where they were mercilessly persecuted for many centuries, just as God had warned they would be. Historically we know this as the Diaspora which began in 70AD when the Romans began to drive Jews from their homeland where they had lived for over a millennium. It wasn't until 1948 that Jews began to return to Israel. God had promised to one day bring them back to the land he had given them.

Whom will *you* honor with your prayers and worship? The Creator or the created?

Our Mediator, our Advocate, is Jesus and only Jesus! It is not Mary, not a priest, not a "saint," and not the Pope. Jesus told us we are to pray to *God the Father*, in his name.

> *"But when you pray, go away by yourself, shut the door*
> *behind you, and pray to your Father in private. Then*
> *your Father, who sees everything, will reward you." –*
> *Matthew 6:6*

There seems to be some confusion on this point. If you look up all of the relevant Scripture verses on the subject, you will discover as I did that we are always directed to pray to God the Father. I admit I was surprised to find that nowhere in the Scriptures are we told to pray to Jesus or to the Holy Spirit. However, since the Bible is silent on this matter, I would not say it is wrong to pray to Jesus or the Holy Spirit, after all, they are part of the Holy Trinity and are therefore one with God the Father. But we are most certainly *not* to pray to anyone but God!

Jesus said...

> *"At that time you won't need to ask me for anything. I tell you the truth, <u>you will ask the Father directly, and he will grant your request because you use my name</u>. You haven't done this before. Ask, using my name, and you will receive, and you will have abundant joy. I have spoken of these matters in figures of speech, but soon I will stop speaking figuratively and will tell you plainly all about the Father. Then you will ask in my name. I'm not saying I will ask the Father on your behalf, for the Father himself loves you dearly because you love me and believe that I came from God." – John 16:23-27*

> *Next the devil took him* (Jesus) *to the peak of a very high mountain and showed him all the kingdoms of the world and their glory. "I will give it all to you," he said, "if you will kneel down and worship me." "Get out of here, Satan," Jesus told him. "For the Scriptures say, <u>'You must worship the Lord your God and serve only him.'"</u> – Matthew 4:8-10*

St. Peter Fourier

St. Peter of Alcantara

St. Camillus de Lellis

St. Lucy Fillipinni

St. Louis de Montfort

St. Anthony Zaccaria

St. Ignatius Loyola

St. Francis of Paola

St. John Bosco

26

St John de la Salle

St John Eudes

St Madeleine Barat

St Philip Neri

St Vincent de Paul

St Teresa of Jesus

St William

St Angela Merici

St Paul of the Cross

St. Bonfilius Monaldi

St Norbert

St Juliana Falconieri

St Bruno

St. Joseph Calasanctius

St Joan Thouret

St. Frances Cabrini

St. Mary Pellettier

St Louis Marillac

St. Jerome Emiliani

St. Cajetan Thiene

St. John of God

St. Peter Nolasco

St. Frances of Rome

St. Alphonsus of Liguori

St Francis Caracciolo

St. Francis de Sales

St Benedict

St. Francis of Assisi   St. Dominic   St. Elijah

The Veneration of Places and Things

A relic, such as a piece of the cross Jesus was crucified on, holds no spiritual value or power whatsoever. To honor such a relic by reverently kissing it with the idea that it in some way holds the power to bless you is to dishonor God.

I have witnessed Catholics kissing relics, genuflecting and making the sign of the cross before statutes, ritualistically lighting candles, kneeling before the Pope and kissing his ring, superstitiously rubbing the feet of a statute of the Apostle Peter, and even kissing the steps and the door of a place they consider "holy." These misplaced affections must certainly offend our God. How can anyone plead ignorance when God's Word is so clear on the subject?

It has been said that we were all created with a God-sized hole in our hearts that only he can fill. I believe this, but not literally of course. God wants to fill that void; he doesn't want us to try to fill it with the veneration of people, places and things, nor does he approve of church leaders who lead people to focus on these things instead of on him.

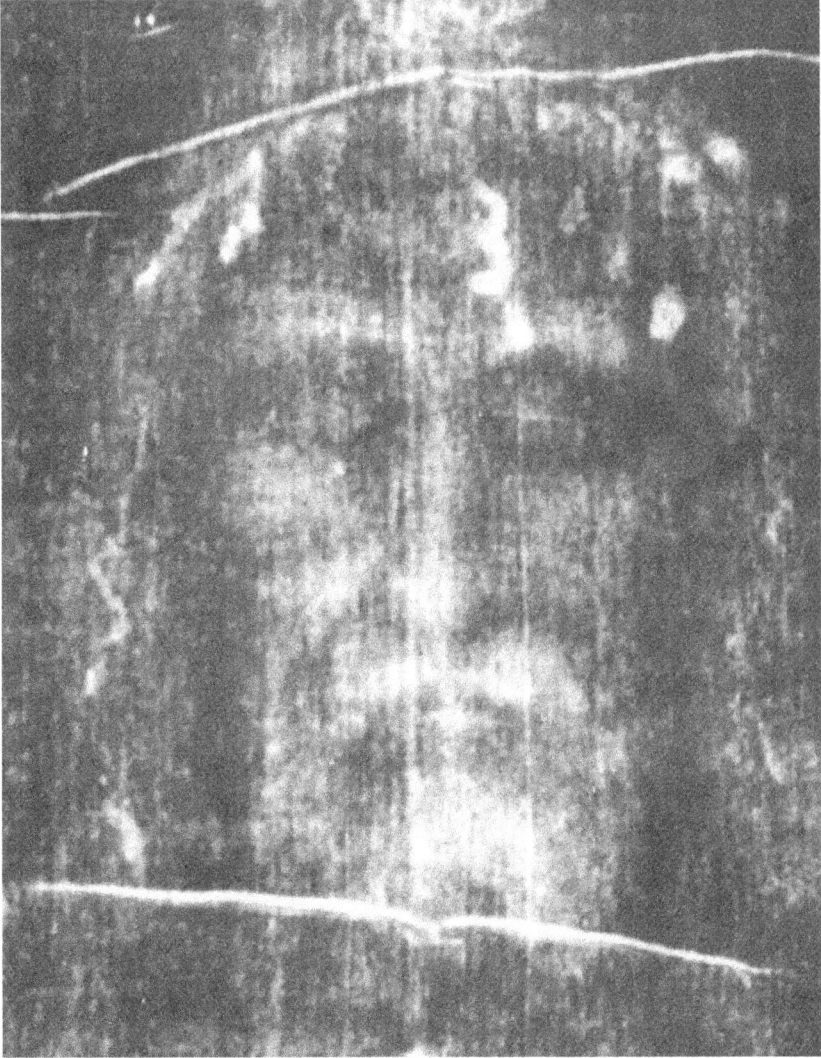

The Shroud of Turin

People superstitiously rubbing the feet of a statue of St. Peter

Chapter 3

Misdirection of the Church's Faithful

The Supremacy of the Church

Approximately 1.2 billion precious souls identify themselves as Catholics. Some are the faithful who continue to diligently seek God within the Catholic Church.

Then there are those who may have attended Catholic school and/or went to mass at one time, but stopped going because the Church didn't seem relevant to them and their daily lives.

Of course many of those 1.2 billion never attended mass regularly, they do not go to confession, and do not pray or read the Bible except on infrequent occasions. Catholicism may have been the faith of their mother and father and of their mothers and fathers, perhaps for generations, but they are not practicing Catholics.

Worldwide the percentage of those who regularly attend mass, even in predominantly Catholic countries, is falling like a stone.

The Catholic Church's primary goal is and always has been to draw people into a relationship with *the Church*, as opposed to a personal relationship with God. For centuries, the Catholic Church has imbued itself with the trappings of authority and power that kept the populous in awe and acceptance that the Church's authority was given to it by God.

We are naturally intimidated by trappings of power and authority

One tactic that helps the Church maintain an aura of legitimacy is keeping people intellectually and spiritually intimidated. There is a Catholic lexicon with close to *two thousand* terms directly or indirectly dealing with Catholicism, worship, morals, history, canon law and spirituality. If you are a Catholic, you may ask yourself, "If I don't even understand the vocabulary of the Church, who am I to question the actions, directives and pronouncements of priests, bishops, archbishops, cardinals and the pope himself?"

"These men wear ultra-expensive robes, stoles, crosses and pointy hats. They carry golden staffs with gold crosses on top. Surely they must know much more than I do about spiritual matters."

34

Traditionally masses were conducted in Latin, so the laity (non-clergy) had little idea of what was being said. It was all rather mysterious and spiritual sounding. It wasn't until November 29, 1964 that the first mass was offered in English in the United States...mixed with some Latin. To help with the time frame, this coincided with the invasion of the United States by the Beatles (the Fab Four from England, not a biblical plague of insects).

When it comes to reading the Bible, the Catholic Church has not actively encouraged Catholics to read and study God's Word. In fact, I think it is fair to say that most Catholic clergy are more conversant about the doctrines, pronouncements and positions of the Catholic Church than they are about Biblical Scripture.

So, if you are one who reads the Bible and knows what it actually says, you may very well know more about who God is and what he is like than those men in ultra-expensive robes, with pointy hats, carrying golden staffs.

For centuries the Church leaders of the time were either not well informed on what the Bible said, or they figured that no one was going to actually read the Bible because it was only in Latin and there were no plans to translate it into the language of the people. Besides, the printing press had not yet been invented, so no one could go to their local Bible bookstore and pick up a copy. That would have caused all kinds of problems. It would have opened the door for parishioners to challenge the things the Church was telling them.

God's word encourages our personal study of the Scriptures. It is from his Word that faith grows; the Bible says faith comes by hearing (and reading) the word of God. It is through his word that the Holy Spirit communicates God's will and thoughts to us and changes our hearts and the direction of our lives. This is known as the process of sanctification. God blesses us through his Word because, as we begin to conform our lives and our thoughts to his, he is free to pour out his blessings on us.

> *All Scripture is inspired by God and is useful to teach us what is true and to make us realize what is wrong in our lives. It corrects us when we are wrong and teaches us to do what is right. God uses it to prepare and equip his people to do every good work. – 2 Timothy 3:16-17.*

> *For the word of God is alive and powerful. It is sharper than the sharpest two-edged sword, cutting between soul and spirit, between joint and marrow. It exposes our innermost thoughts and desires. – Hebrews 4:12*

The living God wants the personal relationship he intended to have with us from the beginning. He wants us to learn about him from his Word, the Bible, and to talk to him in prayer. He wants us to go to his throne as a child goes to his or her loving father and make our requests known to him.

In his book *Jesus Called – He Wants His Church Back*, best-selling author and pastor Rev. Ray Johnston says,

*"...the most startling thing Jesus said was His stunning three-word invitation to **all** people at all times, **'Come to me'** (Matthew 11:28). Notice he didn't say, 'Come to religion,' 'Come to rituals and rules,' 'Come to catechism,' 'Come to confirmation,' 'Come to*

*liturgy.' All those things may be fine and good, but they are **not** the main thing. The main thing is this: **'Come to me.'** Jesus' primary invitation is to a **relationship**! When we miss this, we end up going through the motions and miss the life-giving relationship that is the heart of the Christian faith."*

The Pope

In furtherance of the Church's end to be seen as God's chosen representatives on earth, it was claimed that the authority as head of the Church was first given by God to Peter, one of the Apostles, and that Peter passed down that authority to the next head of the Church, and that it has been passed down successively from one man to the next ever since. These men became known as Popes.

St. Peter died in Rome, and ever since then the Bishop of Rome has been the Pope. When one Pope dies, Cardinals elect his successor. There have been 266 Popes so far. The laity is to believe that each of those men were authorized by God to speak on his behalf and to hand down edicts that were often in conflict with the inspired Word of God as found in Holy Scriptures.

Since 1200 the Church has called this man the Vicar of Christ, meaning Christ's representative on earth. They declared that his spiritual pronouncements are infallible and must be obeyed by all believers who wish to be right with God.

The Scriptures quoted as evidence that Jesus appointed Peter to be the head of the Christian church are highly questionable. To draw that conclusion, and further, to then conclude that Peter passed that authority down, requires that the texts be torturously stretched beyond credulity. That is why there is not a single protestant denomination that believes that Jesus bestowed that authority on Peter. If fact, most of the specific words in contention were probably not addressed to Peter alone, but to all of Jesus' disciples who were present.

Jesus himself, not Peter is the foundation of his church. Peter acknowledged this fact.

> *You are coming to Christ, who is the living cornerstone of God's temple. He was rejected by people, but he was chosen by God for great honor. – 1 Peter 2:4*

Many other Scriptures make it clear that the foundation of the Christian church is Jesus Christ. Saint Paul writes:

> *Because of God's grace to me, I have laid the foundation like an expert builder. Now others are building on it. But whoever is building on this foundation must be very careful. <u>For no one can lay any foundation other than the one we already have – Jesus Christ.</u> – 1 Corinthians 3:10-11*

There is a beautiful old hymn entitled, The Church's One Foundation. The first stanza goes like this:

> The Church's one foundation
> Is Jesus Christ her Lord,
> She is His new creation
> By water and the Word.
> From heaven He came and sought her

To be His holy bride;
With His own blood He bought her
And for her life He died.

Catholics routinely address this man as Holy Father, even though Jesus said...

"And don't address anyone here on earth as 'Father,' for only God in heaven is your spiritual Father." – *Matthew 23:9*

A pope being carried in a gestatorial chair

A Little about Peter

Peter was a good-hearted, sincere and impetuous follower of Jesus. He, along with James and John are the disciples most often mentioned as being with Jesus on various occasions. But like all of us, Peter had his weaknesses. It was very shortly after Peter's wonderful confession of faith (that Jesus was the Messiah and the Son of God) that Jesus had to admonish him. Jesus had just explained that it was necessary that he go to Jerusalem and that there he would be tried and put to death…but that he would rise again three days later. Impetuous Peter took issue with this plan and said so.

> *But Peter took him aside and began to reprimand him for saying such things. "Heaven forbid, Lord," he said.*

41

> *"This will never happen to you!" Jesus turned to Peter and said, "Get away from me, Satan! You are a dangerous trap to me. You are seeing things merely from a human point of view, not from God's." – Matthew 16:22-23*

By calling Peter Satan, Jesus was simply telling Peter that Satan was using him to tempt him to sidestep the ultimate purpose for which he had been born…to die for the sins of the world. Remember, even though Jesus was the Son of God, he had set aside his deity and taken the form of a human being (Philippians 2: 6-8). He did not need Peter or anyone else attempting to shake his resolve.

Peter was married. He had a mother-in-law.

> *When Jesus arrived at Peter's house, <u>Peter's mother-in-law</u> was sick in bed with a high fever. But when Jesus touched her hand, the fever left her. Then she got up and prepared a meal for him. – Matthew 8:14-15*

And Paul wrote:

> *Don't we have the right to bring a Christian wife with us as the other apostles and the Lord's brother do, <u>and as Peter does?</u> - 1 Corinthians 9:5*

Peter is the disciple that walked on water. He and the other disciples saw Jesus walking on the water on the Sea of Galilee one stormy night. As he approached their boat Peter said, "If it is you Lord, bid me to come to you on the water." Jesus said, "Come."

Peter got out of the boat and began to walk toward Jesus. When he saw the strong wind and the waves, he was terrified and began to sink. He shouted,

> *"Save me, Lord. Jesus immediately reached out and grabbed him. "You have so little faith," Jesus said. "Why did you doubt me?" – Matthew 14:31*

While Jesus apparently didn't understand Peter's doubts, I think we can all agree that he exhibited more faith than we could probably muster under the circumstances. To my knowledge, he is the only human who has actually walked on water, albeit for a very short time. This speaks volumes of his faith in Jesus.

Praying the Rosary

The Catholic Church strongly advocates praying the Rosary. You may have seen bumper stickers as I have, probably displayed by devout Catholics, that say, "Pray the Rosary."

Praying the Rosary consists of ritualistically repeating a prescribed series words, confessions and prayers. The Apostles Creed (which was not written by any of the Apostles), the Lord's Prayer, called "Our Fathers', Glory Bes and Hail Marys. For those who are not familiar with Catholic Church jargon, here are the words of a Glory Be and a Hail Mary:

Glory Be: "Glory be to the Father, and to the Son, and to the Holy Spirit, as it was in the beginning, is now, and ever shall be, world without end. Amen."

Hail Mary: "Hail Mary, full of grace, the Lord is with thee; blessed are thou among women, and blessed is the fruit of thy womb, Jesus. Holy Mary, Mother of God, pray for us sinners, now and at the hour of our death. Amen."

Today rosaries have 59 beads. There are 6 large beads which call for repeating the Lord's Prayer (Our Fathers) 6 times. There are 53 beads that call for repeating the prayer to Mary (Hail Mary's) 53 times. These are in addition to saying the Apostle's creed and the Glory Be prayers.

A Rosary

I ran across an article on the internet that details how one is to pray the rosary. It is found at: www.dummies.com/religion/christianity/catholicism/how-to-pray-the-rosary/ It is reproduced below in its entirety (in italics).

HOW TO PRAY THE ROSARY

Rosary beads help Catholics count their prayers. More importantly, Catholics pray the rosary as a means of entreaty to ask God for a special favor, such as helping a loved one recover from an illness, or to thank God for blessings received — a new baby, a new job, a new moon.

1. *On the crucifix, make the sign of the cross and then pray the Apostles' Creed.*

   I believe in God, the Father Almighty, Creator of Heaven and earth; and in Jesus Christ, His only Son, Our Lord, Who was conceived by the Holy Ghost, born of the Virgin Mary, suffered under Pontius Pilate, was crucified; died, and was buried. He descended into Hell; the third day He arose again from the dead; He ascended into Heaven, sitteth at the right hand of God, the Father Almighty; from thence He shall come to judge the living and the dead. I believe in the Holy Spirit, the holy Catholic Church, the communion of saints, the forgiveness of sins, the resurrection of the body, and life everlasting. Amen.

2. *On the next large bead, say the Our Father.*

   Our Father, Who art in heaven, hallowed be Thy name; Thy kingdom come; Thy will be done on earth as it is in heaven. Give us this day our daily bread; and forgive us our trespasses as we forgive those who trespass against us; and lead us not into temptation, but deliver us from evil, Amen.

On the following three small beads, pray three Hail Marys.
Hail Mary, full of grace. The Lord is with thee. Blessed art thou
among women, and blessed is the fruit of thy womb, Jesus. Holy
Mary, Mother of God, pray for us sinners, now and at the hour of
our death. Amen.

3. *On the chain, pray the Glory Be.*

    Glory be to the Father, to the Son, and to the Holy Spirit, as it was,
    is now, and ever shall be, world without end. Amen.

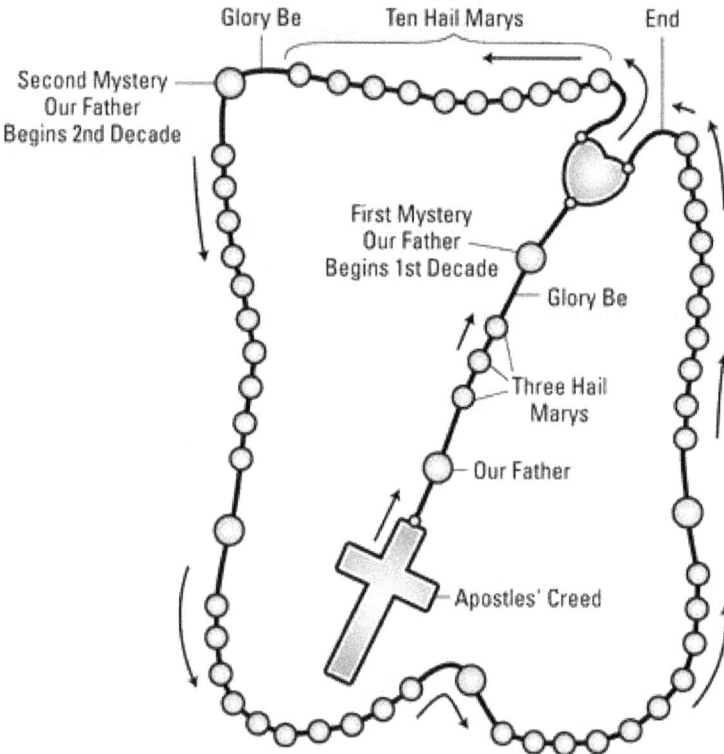

4. *On the large bead, meditate on the first mystery and pray the Our*
    Father.

You pray mysteries for each of the five sections (decades) of the rosary according to the day of the week:

1. *Mondays and Saturdays:*

    The Joyful Mysteries remind the faithful of Christ's birth: The Annunciation (Luke 1:26–38); The Visitation (Luke 1:39–56); The Nativity (Luke 2:1–21); The Presentation (Luke 2:22–38); The Finding of the Child Jesus in the Temple (Luke 2:41–52)

2. *Tuesdays and Fridays:*

    The Sorrowful Mysteries recall Jesus' passion and death: The Agony of Jesus in the Garden (Matthew 26:36–56); The Scourging at the Pillar (Matthew 27:26); The Crowning with Thorns (Matthew 27:27–31); The Carrying of the Cross (Matthew 27:32); The Crucifixion (Matthew 27:33–56).

3. *Wednesdays and Sundays:*

    The Glorious Mysteries focus on the resurrection of Jesus and the glories of heaven: The Resurrection (John 20:1–29); The Ascension (Luke 24:36–53); The Descent of the Holy Spirit (Acts 2:1–41); The Assumption of Mary, the Mother of God, into heaven; The Coronation of Mary in heaven.

4. *Thursdays:*

    Pope John Paul II added The Mysteries of Light, also known as the Luminous Mysteries, in 2002: The Baptism in the River Jordan (Matthew 3:13–16); The Wedding Feast at Cana (John 2:1–11); The Preaching of the coming of the Kingdom of God (Mark 1:14–15); The Transfiguration (Matthew 17:1–8); The Institution of the Holy Eucharist (Matthew 26).

5. *Skip the centerpiece medallion, and on the ten beads after that, pray a Hail Mary on each bead; on the chain, pray a Glory Be.*

Although a decade is 10, these 12 prayers form a decade of the rosary.

Many Catholics add the Fatima Prayer after the Glory Be and before the next Our Father: O My Jesus, forgive us our sins, save us from the fires of hell and lead all souls to heaven, especially those in most need of Thy mercy. Amen.

6. *Repeat Steps 5 and 6 four more times to finish the next four decades.*

7. *At the end of your Rosary, say the Hail Holy Queen.*

Hail, Holy Queen, Mother of mercy, our life, our sweetness, and our hope. To thee do we cry, poor banished children of Eve, to thee do we send up our sighs, mourning and weeping in this valley of tears. Turn then, most gracious advocate, thine eyes of mercy toward us; and after this our exile show unto us the blessed fruit of thy womb Jesus, O clement, O loving, O sweet Virgin Mary.

Pray for us, O holy Mother of God. That we may be made worthy of the promises of Christ.

O God, whose only-begotten Son, by His life, death, and resurrection, has purchased for us the rewards of eternal salvation; grant we beseech Thee, that meditating upon these mysteries of the most holy Rosary of the Blessed Virgin Mary, we may imitate what they contain and obtain what they promise. Through the same Christ our Lord. Amen.

Two Reasons to Never to Pray the Rosary

1. The above article says the Rosary helps a Catholic count their prayers? Count them? God does not want to hear ritualistic repetitions. They do not gain his favor. In fact, I believe these formulaic repetitions are offensive to him. If you are a mother or father, how would you feel if your son or daughter came to you

and ritualistically repeated his or her entreaties over and over in order to gain your favor and move you to respond to their request? They don't need to gain your favor, do they? They already have it. And so it is with God.

> *See how very much our Father loves us, for he calls us his children, and that is what we are! But the people who belong to this world don't recognize that we are God's children because they don't know him. – 1 John 3:1*

Also, Jesus specifically addressed these kinds of prayers.

> *"When you pray, don't babble on and on as the Gentiles do. They think their prayers are answered merely by repeating their words again and again. [8] Don't be like them, for your Father knows exactly what you need even before you ask him! – Matthew 6:7-8*

2. Mary was most blessed by God. She was chosen to bear and help raise the Son of God who set aside his power and glory and came to us as a human being. (See the above section, "The Veneration of Mary".) However, an important point that should be repeated here in connection with the rosary is that Mary is most certainly <u>not</u> the "mother of God." God has existed from eternity; Mary was a human being, and there is nothing in Scripture to suggest that deceased saints can see or hear us.

Mary was not chosen to be a mediator between man and God, that position is held by Jesus alone.

There is one God and one Mediator who can reconcile God and humanity—the man Christ Jesus – 1 Timothy 2:5-6

My dear children, I am writing this to you so that you will not sin. But if anyone does sin, we have an advocate who pleads our case before the Father. He is Jesus Christ, the one who is truly righteous. – 1 John 2:1

Purgatory

The idea behind the Catholic concept of a purgatory is that some people die with minor, pardonable, but unrepented sins, and that the temporal penalty due for sin was not fully paid while they were living. So purgatory is a place of temporary punishment where they are purified so they will be qualified to enter the heaven of a holy God.

To begin with, no one's sins are so minor that they would ever be qualified to enter God's heaven on the basis of merit. It is also true that no one's sins are so heinous that Jesus' blood did not pay the full price for them if that person confesses and sincerely repents of them.

According to this disgraceful doctrine, Jesus' suffering and death on the cross was not entirely sufficient to pay for the sins of the deceased, so additional satisfaction must be paid by the sinner himself. This demeans and cheapens the sacrifice of Jesus Christ.

Jesus, speaking of himself, the Son of God, in the third person, said:

> *"There is no judgment against anyone who believes in him. But anyone who does not believe in him has already been judged for not believing in God's one and only Son."- John 3:18*

He also said,

> *"I tell you the truth, those who listen to my message and believe in God who sent me have eternal life. They will never be condemned for their sins, but they have already passed from death into life. – John 5:24"*

Please note that in these two Scriptures, we are told that there is "no judgment" and "no condemnation" for anyone who believes in Jesus. There is no sin that must still be paid for.

This spurious teaching is heavily based on three verses found in II Maccabees 12:43-45, which is one of the books of the Apocrypha included in Catholic Bibles that is not found in Protestant Bibles. A couple of other Scriptures are also quoted from time to time, but without the Maccabees passages they do not provide any credible support for the doctrine of purgatory.

Protestants do not accept that the Apocryphal books included in the Catholic Bible were written by the inspiration of God. This is very important because if the book itself is of questionable origin and authority, then the scripture passages in it that suggests the possibility of a place such as purgatory cannot be trusted.

Following is part of an email exchange posted on the internet in which Biblical scholar Gary F. Zeolla gives several of the main reasons Protestant Bibles do not include the Apocryphal books (italics):

First, the Jewish canon does not include the Apocrypha. This is significant as it was to the Jews that the OT was entrusted (Rom 3:1,2). Second, some of the Apocrypha books were written in Greek, not Hebrew. So they are distinguished from the Hebrew Scriptures.

Third, Jesus seems to exclude the Apocrypha in his statement in Luke 11:51 – "from the blood of Abel to the blood of Zechariah who perished between the altar and the temple. Yes, I say to you, it shall be required of this generation." NKJV

The death of Abel is recorded in Genesis, the first book in the Hebrew canon. The death of Zechariah is included in 2 Chronicles, the last book in the Hebrew canon (the order of books is different from the order they are in today). So this seems to confirm the Jewish canon as being the correct one.

The order of books as they appear today is taken from the Septuagint (second century BC Greek translation of the OT), which included the Apocrypha. But Jesus is following the Hebrew canon in His statement.

Fourth, no direct quotations from any Apocryphal books appear in the NT. Now there are allusions to Apocryphal events and statements, such 1Maccabees being alluded to in Hebrews 11:37. But none of these allusions rise to the apostles using the Apocrypha as an authoritative source. In other words, there are no Apocrypha quotes in the NT introduced in a way which shows the apostles considered the books to be authoritative, i.e. by using: "It has been written," "spoken by the prophet," "the Holy Spirit spoke," etc.

So with the lack of authoritative quotes from the Apocrypha in the NT, it appears the NT writers, and Jesus Himself, did not accept the Apocrypha as Scripture."

The tragic effect of this teaching of purgatory is that, even in death, Catholics cannot be assured of their eternal salvation. Were their sins here on earth so great that Jesus will reject them completely and send them to hell instead of to purgatory? Or if they were not that bad, how long must they languish in purgatory? How many prayers of their living relatives will be needed to shorten or end their stay, or how much money will have to be paid to the Catholic Church to buy them out? (See the section on Indulgences.)

The Bible gives us many assurances that we are saved when we confess Jesus as Savior and trust in his sacrifice as full payment for our sins. There is nothing additional that we need to pay. No amount of money and no number of prayers contribute anything to our salvation.

> *I have written this to you who believe in the name of the Son of God, so that you may know you have eternal life.*
> *- 1 John 5:13*

So you may <u>know</u> you have eternal life! Not <u>hope</u> that you have eternal life.

And St. Paul leaves no question that our salvation has nothing to do with our merits or good works.

> *God saved you by his grace when you believed. And you can't take credit for this; it is a gift from God. Salvation is not a reward for the good things we have done, so none of us can boast about it. – Ephesians 2:8-9*

He also explains that, through Jesus, we have been reconciled, or made right, with God. God no longer holds our sins against us.

> *This means that anyone who belongs to Christ has become a new person. The old life is gone; a new life has begun! And all of this is a gift from God, who brought us back to himself through Christ. And God has given us this task of reconciling people to him. For God was in Christ, reconciling the world to himself, no longer counting people's sins against them. – 2 Corinthians 5:17-19*

It is Jesus himself who will judge each of us, and he will be judging us on whether we have put our faith and trust in him and the sufficiency of his redeeming sacrifice.

Jesus said:

> *"For just as the Father gives life to those he raises from the dead, so the Son gives life to anyone he wants. In addition, the Father judges no one. Instead, he has*

given the Son absolute authority to judge, so that everyone will honor the Son, just as they honor the Father." - John 5:21-23

One final Scripture from Paul that assures us that our saved souls go directly to be with the Lord when we die:

> *So we are always confident, even though we know that as long as we live in these bodies we are not at home with the Lord. For we live by believing and not by seeing. Yes, we are fully confident, and we would rather be away from these earthly bodies, for then we will be at home with the Lord. – 2 Corinthians 5:6-8*

Chapter 4

Greed and Immorality

The Sale of Indulgences

In the sixteenth century people were told they could buy a pardon from the Catholic Church that would reduce or eliminate their time in purgatory. It is probably safe to assume that if you confessed to murder you would have to pay considerably more for your pardon than if you confessed to adultery or stealing food.

The Church didn't figure on Martin Luther coming along. He was a Catholic priest in Germany who dared to challenge the Papacy on some of its doctrines and greedy, un-Godly practices, like the sale of Indulgences. Sales were booming and money was rolling in the doors of the Church, so Martin did not endear himself to the Church by blowing the whistle on this evil practice. After Luther refused to withdraw condemnation of some of the Church's practices, the Church sought to have him killed to keep him from stirring up the people.

Some who are reading this will be shocked to learn that Indulgences are still for sale by the Catholic Church; however, you can no longer buy them on the street corner. That would spark an uproar that would be devastating to the Church. So now such transactions take place at a much higher level, and only if the reward warrants the risk.

As explained in the Catholic Encyclopedia,

"The pope does not absolve the soul in purgatory from the punishment due his sin, but offers to God from the treasure of the Church whatever may be necessary for the cancelling of this punishment."

This practice is so obviously immoral and controversial that an Indulgence may now only be purchased with the approval of the pope, and provided several conditions are met. One of these conditions, as brazenly stated in the Catholic Encyclopedia, is that there must be "…something pertaining to the glory of God **and the utility of the Church**, not merely the utility accruing to the souls in purgatory."

As I read that, it says that the pardon must not only be for the benefit of the individual, but it must also be worthwhile for the Church.

This brings to mind the opening of the movie Godfather III where Mafia Chieftain Don Corleone receives a high honor bestowed by the Roman Catholic Church...shortly after he donates $100 million to the Church.

I hope I'm not dashing anyone's plans when I say that a pardon by the Catholic Church is totally meaningless. Only God can grant a pardon for sins, and he has already done that...and it's free!

> *For the wages of sin is death, but the **free** gift of God is eternal life through Christ Jesus our Lord. – Romans 6:23*

Sexual Immorality

Studies suggest that the percentage of homosexual priests in the Catholic Church far exceeds that of the general population. In the United States' "politically correct" culture, being actively homosexual has almost become acceptable. While many people change their morals to conform to their culture, God does not. What God declared to be sin, is still sin.

> *I am the Lord, and I do not change. – Malachi 3:6*

We have priests sexually molesting, raping and sodomizing children! How can this be? Men, who presumably had noble aspirations at one time, violating innocent children who have been entrusted into their spiritual care!

For decades, probably more accurately, for centuries, Church leaders, *at the highest levels*, kept horrific tales of abuse out of the public eye through an elaborate culture of secrecy, deception, and intimidation. Victims who came forward with abuse claims were ignored or paid off, while accused priests were quietly transferred from parish to parish or sent for brief periods of psychological counseling. Despite reports of child rape and other criminal behavior by clergymen, Church leaders made no discernible efforts to inform law enforcement authorities.

Jesus, speaking of little children, said,

> *But if you cause one of these little ones who trusts in me to fall into sin, it would be better for you to have a large millstone tied around your neck and be drowned in the depths of the sea. – Matthew 18:6*

There can be little doubt that a significant number of men who chose to take the vow of celibacy did so because their sexual orientation was conflicted. They may have wrestled with homosexual or pedophilic inclinations and, instead of seeking spiritual and psychological counseling, they made the mistake of thinking they could take a vow of celibacy and ignore or suppress those tendencies.

This is not simply a matter of the Church being a cross-section of society. The percentage of homosexual and pedophilic priests in the Church is appalling! The problem is epidemic in proportion! **Many <u>thousands</u> of priests have been accused or convicted of sexually abusing children!** Many more have been implicated, or conspired to sweep these horrendous violations under the carpet. One priest was said to be singularly responsible for molesting over 200 children.

> *The woman wore purple and scarlet clothing and beautiful jewelry made of gold and precious gems and pearls. In her hand she held a gold goblet full of obscenities and the impurities of her immorality. – Revelation 17:4*

No doubt you have heard or read about the widespread cases of abuse in the United States. As early as 2002, some 1,200 priests in the U.S. were accused of abuse, according to a study by *The New York Times*. Many more have been subsequently charged.

This is not just a U.S. phenomenon, it is worldwide. There is hardly a country that has not been scathed by these atrocities committed by Catholic clergymen, with accusations of abuse or the mishandling of scandals forcing the resignation of bishops in Argentina, Germany, Austria, Poland, Ireland, Wales, Scotland, Canada, Australia, Switzerland, and elsewhere.

The following was excerpted from an article dated November 29, 2009 that appeared on the internet under the heading Cultured Views - News, views and commentary. The title of the article is, *The Roman Catholic Church in Ireland: The World's Largest Paedophile Ring Finally Exposed* (italics)

"The most confronting issue for any Roman Catholic has been the revelation that members of our church clergy were responsible for the horrendous and systematic sexual and physical abuse of children on a scale that is almost impossible to comprehend. The exact figures revealing just how many victims there were will never be known because this behaviour has been going on for not years or decades but certainly centuries. We have to come to terms with the fact that the Catholic Church has been the largest paedophile ring in the world with the crimes of these men not restricted to merely Ireland. I prefer not to think of these bastards as priests – they never joined the church to administer the sacraments or serve God and spread his word – they joined simply to have access to innocent children. They were paedophiles first and foremost, never true members of the clergy. And like the three monkeys pictured, the Vatican conspired to see nothing, hear nothing and do absolutely nothing."

Imagine God's anger with those who have brought this great shame upon his Holy Name, and with those at the highest levels of the Catholic Church who have covered up these heinous

crimes and repeatedly moved guilty priests from place to place to shield them from prosecution and punishment!

> *It is a terrible thing to fall into the hands of the living God. – Hebrews 10:31*

The number of victims is unknown, but most likely upwards of one hundred thousand young lives have been damaged or destroyed by these monstrous acts performed by men who held themselves out to be representatives of God!

Listen to what Saint Paul had to say to the Jewish religious leaders of his day:

> *"You who call yourselves Jews are relying on God's law, and you boast about your special relationship with him. You know what he wants; you know what is right because you have been taught his law. You are convinced that you are a guide for the blind and a light for people who are lost in darkness. You think you can instruct the ignorant and teach children the ways of God. For you are certain that God's law gives you complete knowledge and truth.*
>
> *Well then, if you teach others, why don't you teach yourself? You tell others not to steal, but do you steal? Your say it is wrong to commit adultery, but do you commit adultery? You condemn idolatry, but do you use items stolen from pagan temples? You are so proud of knowing the law, but you dishonor God by breaking it.*

> *No wonder the Scriptures say, "The Gentiles blaspheme*
> *the name of God because of you." – Romans 2:17-24*

Now, let's change just a few words and see what Paul might say to the hierarchy of the Catholic Church today…

> *"You who call yourselves **priests, bishops, and cardinals** are relying on God's law, and you boast about your special relationship with him. You know what he wants; you know what is right because you have been taught his law. You are convinced that you are a guide for the blind and a light for people who are lost in darkness. You think you can instruct the ignorant and teach children the ways of God. For you are certain that God's law gives you complete knowledge and truth.*
>
> *Well then, if you teach others, why don't you teach yourself? You tell others not to steal, but do you steal? Your say it is wrong to commit adultery, but do you **sexually abuse innocent children?** You condemn idolatry, but do you **bow down and pray to statues and call upon the dead to help you**? You are so proud of knowing the law, but you dishonor God by breaking it. No wonder the Scriptures say, "The Gentiles blaspheme the name of God because of you."*

I recently heard a woman say that she no longer felt good about confessing her sins to a priest. She speculated that his sins may be worse than her own. She said she had decided she was going to confess her sins directly to God. I can imagine God smiling and maybe even clapping his hands!

What Went Wrong?

"Sanctification" is the biblical term that refers to the process by which we become more and more like God in our thoughts, actions and attitudes as we grow in our personal relationship with him.

God's Word is truth, and we become sanctified (grow in holiness) as we read and study his Word.

I think it is safe to say that it is a rare priest who studies God's Word daily. Even as the Church's "faithful" have been misled, so too have priests been misled into thinking their primary relationship should be with the Church instead of with God himself. Anyone who is not cultivating his relationship with God is especially vulnerable to all sorts of sinful temptations.

Jesus, praying to God the Father about his disciples and those who would believe in him in the future (us), prayed,

> *"Make them holy by your truth; <u>teach them your word,</u> <u>which is truth</u>. Just as you sent me into the world, I am sending them into the world. And I give myself as a holy sacrifice for them <u>so they can be made holy by your</u> <u>truth</u>." – John 17:17-19*

Saint Paul had this to say about sexual sin:

> *God's will is for you to be holy, so stay away from all sexual sin. Then each of you will control his own body*

and live in holiness and honor – not in lustful passion like the pagans who do not know God and his ways. – 1 Thessalonians 4:3-5

Avoiding sexual sin, or any strong temptation, is not a matter of willpower. It is desirable to seek to live in a manner that pleases God, but it cannot be done by willpower. St. Paul makes it apparent that we are overmatched in such struggles.

> *For we are not fighting against flesh-and-blood enemies, but against evil rulers and authorities of the unseen world, against mighty powers in this dark world, and against evil spirits in heavenly places. – Ephesians 6:12*

Paul goes on to warn us to put on every piece of God's armor so we will be able to resist sinful temptations, and so that after the battle, we will still be standing firm.

> *Stand your ground, putting on the belt of truth and the body armor of God's righteousness. For shoes, put on the peace that comes from the Good News so that you will be fully prepared. In addition to all of these, hold up the shield of faith to stop the fiery arrows of the devil. – Ephesians 6:14-16*

And finally we are to:

> *Put on salvation as your helmet, and <u>take the sword of the Spirit, which is the word of God</u>. – Ephesians 6:17*

The backbone of our relationship with God always comes back to knowing his Word.

Condoning the Worship of Other "Deities"

The Roman Catholic Church does not directly participate in satanic rituals or worship, however, in much of the world she condones millions of her members participating in satanic ceremonies in which other deities and spirits are worshipped. On a typical Sunday people may attend morning mass, and that evening participate in reprehensible ceremonies that are offensive to God.

The Church hierarchy would rather retain members, their power base and source of income, than alienate them by demanding they make a choice between worshipping the one true God and the pluralistic worship of multiple "deities" and lesser spirits. Power and financial revenue has proven more important to the Catholic Church than the spiritual condition and eternal salvation of the people.

In Haiti and other Caribbean countries it is **Voodoo** or Vodou, a fusion of Roman Catholic ritual elements and the animism and magic of Africa in which a supreme God rules a large pantheon of deities, deified ancestors, and Catholic saints, who communicate with worshippers via dreams, trances, and demonic possessions. A priest or priestess leads worshipers in ceremonies involving singing, dancing, drumming, prayer, and sacrifices - both animal and *human!*

The first democratically elected president of Haiti, Jean-Bertrand Aristide, was a Catholic priest before being elected president. As President he personally participated in voodoo ceremonies and publicly encouraged the practice of voodoo, both in speeches and by way of financial support from the government.

His successor, President Rene Preval, is widely believed to have participated in voodoo ceremonies inside the presidential palace that involved sacrificing children.

There is a saying in Haiti: "85% of Haitians are Catholic, but all of them practice voodoo." While that is an exaggeration, it gives you an idea of their religious culture.

He gave a mighty shout: "Babylon is fallen—that great city is fallen! She has become a home for demons. She is a hideout for every foul[a] spirit, a hideout for every foul vulture and every foul and dreadful animal. –
Revelation 18:2

66

Santería is a religious movement that originated in Cuba. It has spread to Latin America. It combines West African beliefs and practices with elements of Roman Catholicism. It includes belief in one supreme being, but worship and rituals center on deities or patron saints (with parallels among Roman Catholic saints). Practices may include trance dancing, rhythmic drumming, (demonic) spirit possession, and animal sacrifice.

In Brazil it is **Macumba,** an Afro-Brazilian religion characterized by a fusion of African religions, Brazilian spiritualism and Roman Catholicism. African elements include the sacrifice of animals, spirit offerings, and dances. Macumba rites are led by mediums who fall prostrate in trances and communicate with "holy" spirits. Roman Catholic elements include the cross and the worship of saints, who are given African names.

This is where Godly church leaders are obligated to exercise every bit of influence they have over their church members. This is where they need to take a stand and say, "No! This is wrong. You cannot be a member of our church and also worship other 'gods!' You must choose!" The response of the Catholic Church clergy has been…………………….. (silence)

In the 1700s Haiti was France's richest colony and was known as the Pearl of the Antilles for its singular beauty. The populace consisted of slaves who had been brought to Haiti from Africa. The indigenous people had died off from illnesses for which they had no immunity. In 1791 a group of voodoo priests made a pact with the devil. If he would help them liberate Haiti from the rule of the French, they would dedicate the country to Satan for 200 years.

The subsequent uprising was successful and Haiti became a nation in 1804.

Not surprisingly, Haiti is now the poorest country in the western hemisphere. Unemployment is above 80%. Most of the trees have been cut down. Erosion has washed the once fertile soils into the ocean. In some places people eat seasoned, dried mud patties just to ease their hunger pangs. Jesus warned that the devil comes to kill, steal and destroy.

Haiti's problems appear on the surface to be economic, but they are in fact spiritual.

The home of a voodoo priest in Haiti

Chapter 5

Our Relationship with God

Our Sinful Nature

When the Bible speaks of a person, people, place or thing as being holy, it usually means, "Set apart for God." In the King James Version of the Bible there is a passage that speaks of God inspiring the Holy Scriptures. It says,

> *For the prophecy came not in old time by the will of man: but **holy** men of God spake as they were moved by the Holy Ghost. – 2 Peter 1:21 (KJV)*

As used here, "holy men of God" refers to them being set apart for a special purpose for which God chose them. It does not mean that they were perfect and without sin.

Similarly, the children of Israel were instructed:

> *And thou shalt make **holy** garments for Aaron thy brother for glory and for beauty. – Exodus 28:2 (KJV)*

Of course this does not mean that the garments would be without sin, but that they were to be special and set aside for God's purposes.

We who have invited Jesus to be the Lord of our lives are called to be holy. That is, we are challenged to live blameless lives with the help of the Holy Spirit who lives within us.

> *So you must live as God's obedient children. Don't slip back into your old ways of living to satisfy your own desires. You didn't know any better then. But now you must be holy in everything you do, just as God who chose you is holy. For the Scriptures say, "You must be holy because I am holy." 1 Peter 1:14-16*

Besides for Adam and Eve before the fall, the only one mentioned in the Bible who is sinless, is God, including God the Son, Jesus Christ.

Abraham, Isaac and Jacob of the Old Testament, along with Mary, Peter, Paul and the writers of the four gospels in the New Testament, were all sinners like you and me.

Saint Paul, who is credited with writing more than half of the books in the New Testament (by the inspiration of the Holy Spirit), had this to say about himself:

> *"And I know that nothing good lives in me, that is, in my sinful nature. I want to do what is right, but I can't. I want to do what is good, but I don't. I don't want to do what is wrong, but I do it anyway. But if I do what I don't want to do, I am not really the one doing wrong; it is sin living in me that does it.*

I have discovered this principle of life – that when I want to do what is right, I inevitably do what is wrong. I love God's law with all my heart. But there is another power within me that is at war with my mind. This power makes me a slave to the sin that is still within me. Oh, what a miserable person I am! Who will free me from this life that is dominated by sin and death?" – Romans 7:18-24

Then he answers his own question.

"Thank God! The answer is in Jesus Christ our Lord." – Romans 7:25

We might call Paul a "holy" man of God from the perspective that he was chosen by God and set apart to preach and teach the Word of God. But we cannot call him sinless. By his own admission he was not.

Guilt, Penance and Good Works

Martin Luther, the rebellious German monk, often felt overwhelmed by the virulence of his sinful nature. He confessed his sins obsessively and even flagellated himself in an effort to bring his sinful body under his control, to no avail.

We are all born with a sinful nature that will lead us to sin. From his study of the Scriptures, Martin Luther discovered that he was fighting a losing battle, but that God does not expect us to live sinless lives. He knows we cannot. It was for that very reason he sent his blameless Son to pay the full price for our sins. Because of

Jesus' sacrifice for us, God sees us as righteous! His Word tells us that he has removed our sins from us as far as the east is from the west. He sees us as holy! **Yes, you and me, holy!**

Martin voiced his discovery to the Catholic Church and took issue with their emphasis on the importance of doing good works, of doing penance, and/or paying large sums of money to the Church to gain favor with God. Luther's study of the Scriptures told him that people are saved from their sins by God's grace and mercy alone.

We cannot do anything to earn God's love and forgiveness. It is a free gift from a loving and merciful God.

> *God saved you by his grace when you believed. And you can't take credit for this; it is a gift from God. Salvation is not a reward for the good things we have done, so none of us can boast about it. – Ephesians 2:8-9*

The whole idea of "penance" comes from the mind of men, not God. It is man striving to find favor with God by doing something that will appease him and turn away his wrath. But the God who has revealed himself to us in the Bible is not like that. He is a God of mercy and compassion who is ready to forgive all who come to him in the name of his Son, Jesus Christ.

Listen to how God describes himself:

> *Then the Lord came down in a cloud and stood there with him (Moses); and he called out his own name, Yahweh. The Lord passed in front of Moses, calling out,*

> *"Yahweh! The Lord! The God of compassion and mercy! I am slow to anger and filled with unfailing love and faithfulness. I lavish unfailing love to a thousand generations. I forgive iniquity, rebellion, and sin." - Exodus 34:5-7*

And this is how Saint Paul describes the incredible love of God:

> *And may you have the power to understand, as all God's people should, how wide, how long, how high, and how deep his love is. May you experience the love of Christ, though it is too great to understand fully. - Ephesians 3:18-19*

And he writes,

> *But God showed his great love for us by sending Christ to die for us while we were still sinners. - Romans 5:8*

In other words, God didn't say, "Clean up your act and then come see me." He paid for our sins himself and then invites us to receive his free gift of eternal life by trusting in his Son's sacrifice as full payment for our sins.

Once we have made Jesus the Lord of our life, we will not willfully continue to commit sins that we know are displeasing to him. And when we slip, we need only acknowledge our failure and ask for forgiveness.

> *But if we confess our sins to him, he is faithful and just*
> *to forgive us our sins and to cleanse us from all*
> *wickedness. - 1 John 1:9*

As Saint Paul says, we are no longer our own, we were bought with the price of Jesus' blood.

Can We Ever Be Sure of Our Salvation?

So many people are uncertain about their salvation. As we have discussed in the Purgatory section, there is nothing we can do that will contribute to our salvation. Jesus paid the full penalty for our sins, and there is nothing more to do to make ourselves right with God.

But then we read in the Bible,

> *Don't you realize that those who do wrong will not*
> *inherit the Kingdom of God? Don't fool yourselves.*
> *Those who indulge in sexual sin, or who worship idols,*
> *or commit adultery, or are male prostitutes, or practice*
> *homosexuality, or are thieves or greedy people, or*

74

drunkards, or are abusive, or cheat people – none of these will inherit the Kingdom of God. – 1 Corinthians 6:9-10

…and we again begin to question our salvation. Are we good enough?

St. Paul continues…

> *Some of you were once like that. But you were cleansed; you were made holy; you were made right with God by calling on the name of the Lord Jesus Christ and by the Spirit of God. – 1 Corinthians 6:11*

So our sins are forgiven no matter how bad they were, but what about the sins we continue to commit? Certainly we cannot willfully continue to sin and expect God to continue to forgive us, can we? No, we can't. We will all continue to sin as long as we live in these sinful, earthly bodies, but when we do so <u>willfully</u>, we need to repent and confess that sin. Confession is nothing more than acknowledging to God that we did something wrong and asking for forgiveness. If our confession and repentance are sincere, God will never fail to forgive us and restore the relationship we violated by our willfulness. On the other hand…

> *Dear friends, if we deliberately continue sinning after we have received knowledge of the truth, there is no longer any sacrifice that will cover these sins. There is only the terrible expectation of God's judgment and the raging fire that will consume his enemies. - Hebrews 10:26-27*

The Bible tells us that believing in Jesus Christ gives us the right to be called God's children and the right to go to his throne and talk to him in prayer the way a son or daughter talks to a father whom they know loves them. That new relationship is intended to last forever. Jesus said he will never allow Satan to snatch us out of his hands.

A relationship much like God's institution of marriage

In a way it is like the institution of marriage. After we leave the altar, we are married. It's official! The new relationship is intended to be permanent. The marital relationship will inevitably experience its ups and downs. There are times we will offend our partner. Perhaps we will forget our partner's birthday or become so engrossed in other things that we cease to spend personal time with him or her. We may make our partner jealous or angry by something we do. We may even be unfaithful to our partner and cause great offense. BUT, through it all **we continue to be married**; we continue to be in that special relationship. If we are sorry for our shortcomings, and if our partner has a forgiving nature like God does, he or she will forgive us for all the things we do wrong, and will continue to love us. The relationship remains unbroken.

At the moment we cross the faith threshold and believe that Jesus died for our sins and confess him as Lord, the Holy Spirit takes up residence inside of us. At that instant we have entered into a saving relationship with God that is very much like the marital relationship. God knows there will be ups and downs. We will offend him. We may make him jealous by the way we use our time and the things we make our priorities. We may fall into sins of the flesh. We may even be completely unfaithful to him for a time, but the relationship continues. **We have not lost our salvation!** God will patiently work to draw us to repentance because he wants the relationship to remain intact. The only way God will give up on the relationship is if <u>we</u> no longer value it. If <u>we</u> insist on going our own way and refuse to work at the relationship there will come a time that his patience will run out…and his Holy Spirit will leave us. <u>We</u> will have broken the relationship by showing our contempt for it.

I like to say that we need to make Jesus **"the Lord of our life."** What that means to me is that not only do we trust in his death on the cross as full payment for our sins, but we also seek to please him in our daily lives because we are no longer our own, he bought us with the price of his precious blood. We owe him everything.

Once we are in a relationship with the living God, we must do our part to keep that relationship healthy. Here are four things we should do to protect our new relationship:

1.   **Read the Bible** and let God speak to us through his Word. It is through the Bible that we come to know God more intimately and begin to understand his character and his amazing love for us. His Word has the power to transform our lives and change us from the inside out.
2.   **Talk to God** in prayer. Every relationship requires two-way communication. He wants to hear from us. He wants us to ask him for what we need and to thank him for all he does for us. He hears and answers the prayers of his children.
3.   **Be careful in our choice of close friends**. The Bible tells us that bad company corrupts good character. If we may be tempted to use drugs, we should not hang out with people who

use or sell drugs. If we are especially vulnerable to sexual temptation, we will need to stay away from those who may encourage us to sin sexually.

4.   **Tell others about Jesus** and about our relationship with God. It is his desire that all people come to him and be saved. He has given us the responsibility to tell others.

By doing these four things, we invest in our relationship with God, and Satan will not be able to come between us.

God called King David a man after his own heart. Listen to this prayer from David's heart.

> *How can I know all the sins lurking in my heart? Cleanse me from these hidden faults. Keep your servant from deliberate sins! Don't let them control me. Then I will be free of guilt and innocent of great sin. May the words of my mouth and the meditation of my heart be pleasing to you, O Lord, my rock and my redeemer. Psalm 19:12-14*

So the answer to the question, "Can We Ever Be Sure of Our Salvation?" is a resounding, "Yes! Absolutely!" If we make Jesus the Lord of our life we will spend eternity with him. Our continuing failures to live without sin will not be held against us because Jesus paid the whole penalty for those sins. God sees us as blameless, washed by the blood of his Son.

> *Now all glory to God, who is able to keep you from falling away and will bring you with great joy into his glorious presence without a single fault. – Jude vs. 24*

Reading the Bible

I encourage every reader of this book to regularly read the Bible. You need to know what it says. Carefully check out everything you are told, and if it is not supported in the Bible, you can conclude that what you were told is human thinking which may or may not be valid.

As you read God's Word, ask him to open your mind and help you understand. It's his Word and he gave it for *you*, so he has a vested interest in helping you understand it.

There is great value in reading God's Word.

> *All Scripture is God-breathed and is useful for teaching, rebuking, correcting and training in righteousness, so that the man of God may be thoroughly equipped for every good work. - 2 Timothy 3:16*

In this Scripture, "man of God," does not refer to men in the Church hierarchy. It means *you* and *me*, men and women who are followers of Jesus Christ. We need to know what God's Word says so that we will not be duped by charlatans who come across as speaking for God.

We need to know his will for our lives. He has plans for each of us that were made before we were born, but we need to be on God's wavelength in order to hear from him.

For we are God's masterpiece. He has created us anew in Christ Jesus, so we can do the good things he planned for us long ago. – Ephesians 2:10

Chapter 6

The Church Will Answer to a Holy God

His Righteous Anger

God is loving, kind, merciful and forgiving...with those whom he sees as blameless because of their faith and trust in what Jesus did for them on the cross.

But we must never forget that he is also a holy God who does not tolerate wickedness. And in particular, he does not tolerate those who hold themselves out as his representatives yet disregard his commands or engage is blatant immorality. They are held to a higher standard.

Following are three stories from the Bible that illustrate God's righteous anger against sin. As you will see, his tolerance is very low.

In Leviticus chapter 10 Aaron is the high priest. His sons Nadab and Abihu are also priests. The sons took liberties in how they served God, not following the specific instructions he had given them.

> *Aaron's sons Nadab and Abihu put coals of fire in their incense burners and sprinkled incense over them. In this way, they disobeyed the LORD by burning before him the wrong kind of fire, different than he had commanded. ² So fire blazed forth from the LORD's presence and*

*burned them up, and they died there before the LORD.
³ Then Moses said to Aaron, "This is what the LORD
meant when he said, 'I will display my holiness through
those who come near me. I will display my glory before
all the people.'" And Aaron was silent. ⁴ Then Moses
called for Mishael and Elzaphan, Aaron's cousins, the
sons of Aaron's uncle Uzziel. He said to them, "Come
forward and carry away the bodies of your relatives
from in front of the sanctuary to a place outside the
camp." ⁵ So they came forward and picked them up by
their garments and carried them out of the camp, just
as Moses had commanded. ⁶ Then Moses said to Aaron
and his sons Eleazar and Ithamar, "Do not show grief
by leaving your hair uncombed[a] or by tearing your
clothes. If you do, you will die, and the LORD's anger
will strike the whole community of Israel. However, the
rest of the Israelites, your relatives, may mourn because
of the LORD's fiery destruction of Nadab and Abihu.
⁷ But you must not leave the entrance of the Tabernacle[b]
or you will die, for you have been anointed with the
LORD's anointing oil." So they did as Moses
commanded. – Leviticus 10:1-7*

Next we see God's fierce anger over idol worship.

*The LORD issued the following command to Moses:
"Seize all the ringleaders and execute them before the
LORD in broad daylight, so his fierce anger will turn
away from the people of Israel." ⁵ So Moses ordered
Israel's judges, "Each of you must put to death the men
under your authority who have joined in worshiping
Baal of Peor." ⁶ Just then one of the Israelite men*

brought a Midianite woman into his tent, right before the eyes of Moses and all the people, as everyone was weeping at the entrance of the Tabernacle. [7] When Phinehas son of Eleazar and grandson of Aaron the priest saw this, he jumped up and left the assembly. He took a spear [8] and rushed after the man into his tent. Phinehas thrust the spear all the way through the man's body and into the woman's stomach. So the plague against the Israelites was stopped, [9] but not before <u>*24,000 people had died.*</u> *[10] Then the LORD said to Moses, [11] "Phinehas son of Eleazar and grandson of Aaron the priest has turned my anger away from the Israelites by being as zealous among them as I was. So I stopped destroying all Israel as I had intended to do in my zealous anger. [12] Now tell him that I am making my special covenant of peace with him. [13] In this covenant, I give him and his descendants a permanent right to the priesthood, for in his zeal for me, his God, he purified the people of Israel, making them right with me." – Numbers 25:4-13*

Last, King David greatly angered God by taking a census of all of the men in Israel who were capable of handling a sword. David was looking to human strength for assurance instead of to the Lord who had always been his deliverer. When he realized he had done a very foolish thing, he confessed his sin and asked God to forgive him.

God was very displeased with the census, and he punished Israel for it. [8] Then David said to God, "I have sinned greatly by taking this census. Please forgive my guilt for doing this foolish thing." [9] Then the

LORD *spoke to Gad, David's seer. This was the message:* [10] *"Go and say to David, This is what the* LORD *says: I will give you three choices. Choose one of these punishments, and I will inflict it on you.'"* [11] *So Gad came to David and said, "These are the choices the* LORD *has given you.* [12] *You may choose three years of famine, three months of destruction by the sword of your enemies, or three days of severe plague as the angel of the* LORD *brings devastation throughout the land of Israel. Decide what answer I should give the* LORD *who sent me."* [13] *"I'm in a desperate situation!" David replied to Gad. "But let me fall into the hands of the* LORD, *for his mercy is very great. Do not let me fall into human hands."* [14] *So the* LORD *sent a plague upon Israel, and 70,000 people died as a result.* [15] *And God sent an angel to destroy Jerusalem. But just as the angel was preparing to destroy it, the* LORD *relented and said to the death angel, "Stop! That is enough!" –*
1 Chronicles 21: 7-15

Is God Calling His People to Leave the Roman Catholic Church?

Instead of leading people into a relationship with the living God, the Roman Catholic Church has led untold billions of souls into a relationship with a greedy and corrupt institution that has deceived them with man-made, non-scriptural doctrines.

The book of Revelation contains a lot of imagery that is difficult to understand. Nevertheless, I submit to you that when the clues given in Chapter 7 of this book are pieced together, there can be little doubt that the Great Prostitute spoken of is the Roman Catholic Church. But you will have to decide for yourself.

> *Then I heard another voice calling from heaven, "Come away from her, my people. Do not take part in her sins, or you will be punished with her.* [5] *For her sins are piled as high as heaven, and God remembers her evil deeds. – Revelation 18:4-5*

There are many God loving men and women in the Catholic Church. They have sought God in the Bible and found him. They have a personal relationship with their creator and redeemer. They recognize many of the Church's failings, but may have never seriously thought of leaving her. Some have even tried to reform her from within, with very limited success.

Chapter 7

End-Time Prophecy Clues

In his wisdom God chose to give us clues to the identity of the Great Prostitute described in Revelation chapters 17 and 18. It is up to us to put the clues together to see to whom they point. Here is a quick recap of those clues.

1.   She rules from a city with seven hills known as Babylon
2.   She rules over masses of people of every nation and language
3.   The kings of the earth have committed adultery with her
4.   The blood of God's people is on her hands
5.   Her extravagances have made the merchants of the world rich
6.   Music and the happy voices of brides and grooms will never be heard in her again.

She Rules From a City with Seven Hills

"This calls for a mind with understanding: The seven heads of the beast represent the seven hills where the woman rules. They also represent seven kings. – Revelation 17:9

The City of Rome has always been known as the City of Seven Hills. In fact, footnotes to Revelation 17 in the New American Bible and the Jerusalem Bible, *which are both Catholic translations*, say that the seven hills are the Seven Hills of Rome.

Vatican City is a separate sovereign country nestled in the heart of Rome, the capital city of Italy.

Inside Vatican City is St. Peter's Basilica, the largest church in the world, the Sistine Chapel, the Vatican Museum, the Apostolic Palace which is the Pope's residence, the Palace of the Governorate and the Vatican Library, among other buildings. The Vatican is under the absolute authority of the pope of the Roman Catholic Church.

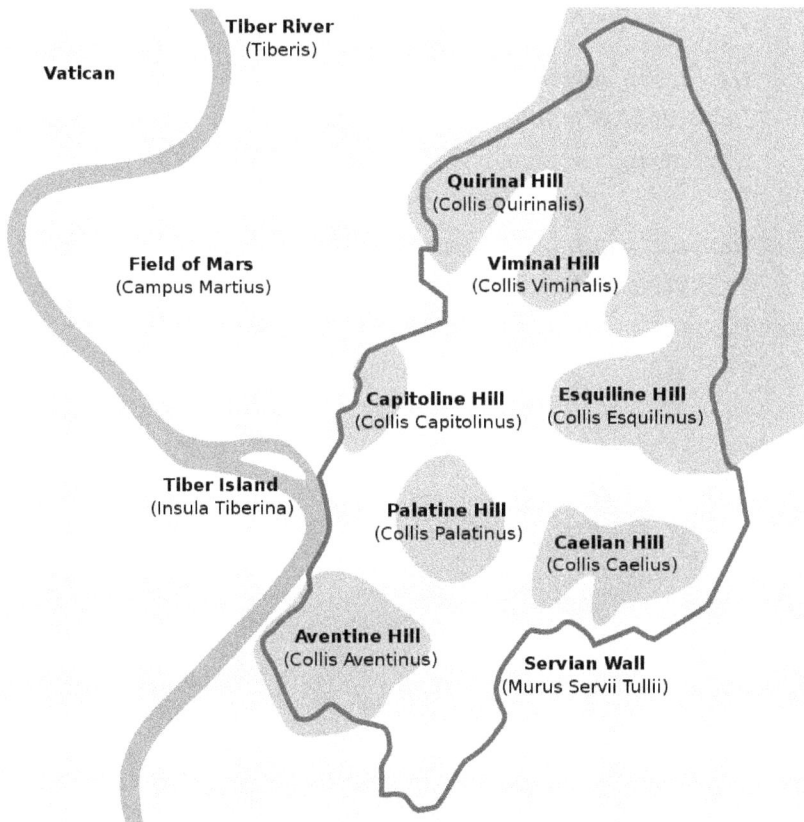

The Seven Hills of Rome

At the time the book of Revelation was written, the early Christians were persecuted by Rome, which was historically known as the "City of Seven Hills."

The Catholic Encyclopedia states:
"It is within the city of Rome, called the city of seven hills, that the entire area of Vatican State proper is now confined."

She Rules Over Masses of People of Every Nation and Language

Then the angel said to me, "The waters where the prostitute is ruling represent masses of people of every nation and language. – Revelation 17:15

The Catholic Church's estimated worldwide membership is about 1.2 billion people...approximately one-sixth of the world's population.

If you have access to a computer, you may want to do a search for one or more of the following:

Roman Catholic Church in Algeria
Roman Catholic Church in Albania
Roman Catholic Church in Andorra
Roman Catholic Church in Angola
Roman Catholic Church in Argentina
Roman Catholic Church in Armenia
Roman Catholic Church in Australia
Roman Catholic Church in Austria
Roman Catholic Church in Bangladesh
Roman Catholic Church in Brunei
Roman Catholic Church in the Bahamas
Roman Catholic Church in Belarus
Roman Catholic Church in Belgium
Roman Catholic Church in Belize
Roman Catholic Church in Bolivia
Roman Catholic Church in Bosnia and Herzegovina
Roman Catholic Church in Brazil
Roman Catholic Church in Bulgaria
Roman Catholic Church in Burma
Roman Catholic Church in Canada
Roman Catholic Church in Chile
Roman Catholic Church in China
Roman Catholic Church in Colombia
Roman Catholic Church in Costa Rica
Roman Catholic Church in Croatia
Roman Catholic Church in Cuba
Roman Catholic Church in the Czech Republic
Roman Catholic Church in Côte d'Ivoire
Roman Catholic Church in Denmark
Roman Catholic Church in Dominica
Roman Catholic Church in the Dominican Republic
Roman Catholic Church in Ecuador
Roman Catholic Church in Egypt
Roman Catholic Church in El Salvador
Roman Catholic Church in Equatorial Guinea
Roman Catholic Church in Estonia

Roman Catholic Church in Ethiopia
Roman Catholic Church in Fiji
Roman Catholic Church in Finland
Roman Catholic Church in France
Roman Catholic Church in French Guiana
Roman Catholic Church in Ghana
Roman Catholic Church in Guatemala
Roman Catholic Church in The Gambia
Roman Catholic Church in Germany
Roman Catholic Church in Guyana
Roman Catholic Church in Haiti
Roman Catholic Church in Honduras
Roman Catholic Church in Hong Kong
Roman Catholic Church in Hungary
Roman Catholic Church in Iceland
Roman Catholic Church in India
Roman Catholic Church in Indonesia
Roman Catholic Church in Iraq
Roman Catholic Church in Ireland
Roman Catholic Church in Israel
Roman Catholic Church in Italy
Roman Catholic Church in Jamaica
Roman Catholic Church in Japan
Roman Catholic Church in Kenya
Roman Catholic Church in Korea
Roman Catholic Church in Lebanon
Roman Catholic Church in Latvia
Roman Catholic Church in Lithuania
Roman Catholic Church in Luxembourg
Roman Catholic Church in Mauritius
Roman Catholic Church in Macau
Roman Catholic Church in Madagascar
Roman Catholic Church in Malaysia
Roman Catholic Church in Mexico
Roman Catholic Church in Namibia
Roman Catholic Church in North Korea
Roman Catholic Church in the Netherlands
Roman Catholic Church in the Netherlands Antilles
Roman Catholic Church in New Zealand
Roman Catholic Church in Nicaragua

Roman Catholic Church in Nigeria
Roman Catholic Church in Norway
Roman Catholic Church in Papua New Guinea
Roman Catholic Church in Pakistan
Roman Catholic Church in Palau
Roman Catholic Church in Panama
Roman Catholic Church in Paraguay
Roman Catholic Church in Peru
Roman Catholic Church in the Philippines
Roman Catholic Church in Poland
Roman Catholic Church in Portugal
Roman Catholic Church in Puerto Rico
Roman Catholic Church in Russia
Roman Catholic Church in South Africa
Roman Catholic Church in Sri Lanka
Roman Catholic Church in the Solomon Islands
Roman Catholic Church in South Korea
Roman Catholic Church in Saint Lucia
Roman Catholic Church in Scotland
Roman Catholic Church in Serbia
Roman Catholic Church in Sierra Leone
Roman Catholic Church in Singapore
Roman Catholic Church in Slovenia
Roman Catholic Church in Spain
Roman Catholic Church in Sweden
Roman Catholic Church in São Tomé and Príncipe
Roman Catholic Church in Taiwan
Roman Catholic Church in Thailand
Roman Catholic Church in Tonga
Roman Catholic Church in Trinidad and Tobago
Roman Catholic Church in Uganda
Roman Catholic Church in the United Kingdom
Roman Catholic Church in the United States
Roman Catholic Church in Uruguay
Roman Catholic Church in Vanuatu
Roman Catholic Church in Venezuela
Roman Catholic Church in Vietnam
Roman Catholic Church in Yemen
Roman Catholic Church in Zambia
Roman Catholic Church in Zimbabwe

The Woman is a City

And this woman you saw in your vision represents the great city that rules over the kings of the world." – Revelation 17:18

The Kings of the World Have Committed Adultery with Her

For all the nations have fallen because of the wine of her passionate immorality. The kings of the world have committed adultery with her. Because of her desires for extravagant luxury, the merchants of the world have grown rich." – Revelation 18:3

The Roman Catholic Church has always been preoccupied with money and power. Her popes have orchestrated immoral but economically beneficial relationships with many of the kings and rulers of the world.

A long line of popes have claimed dominion over the entire Christian world and demanded obedience and the payment of taxes to the Church.

In his book, *A Woman Rides the Beast* © 1994, prophecy researcher Dave Hunt points out that the Bible is clearly talking about spiritual adultery, not the physical kind.

"Fornication and adultery are used in the Bible in both the physical and the spiritual sense. Of Jerusalem God said, "How is the faithful city become a harlot!" (Isaiah 1:21). Israel, whom God had set apart from all other peoples to be holy for His purposes, had entered into unholy, adulterous alliances with the idol-worshiping nations about her. There is no way that a city could engage in literal, fleshly fornication. Thus we can only conclude that John, like the prophets in the Old Testament, is using the term in its spiritual sense. The city, therefore, must claim a spiritual relationship with God. Otherwise such an allegation would be meaningless."

Dave Hunt goes on to tell about the Catholic Church's worldwide political philandering:

"Pope Alexander VI (1492-1503) claimed that all undiscovered lands belonged to the Roman Pontiff, for him to dispose of as he pleased in the name of Christ as His vicar. King John II of Portugal was convinced that in his Bull Romanus Pontifex the pope had granted all that Columbus discovered exclusively to him and his country. Ferdinand and Isabel of Spain, however, thought the pope had given the same lands to them. In May 1493 the Spanish-born Alexander VI issued three bulls to settle the dispute.

In the name of Christ, who had no place on this earth that He called his own, this incredibly evil Borgia pope, claiming to own the world, drew a north-south line down the global map of that day, giving everything on the east to Portugal and on the west to Spain. Thus by papal grant, "out of the plenitude of apostolic power," Africa went to Portugal and the Americas to Spain. When Portugal "succeeded in reaching India and Malaya, they secured the confirmation of these discoveries from the Papacy..." There was a condition, of course: "to the intent to bring the inhabitants ... to profess the Catholic Faith." It was largely Central and South America which, as a consequence of this unholy alliance between church and state, had Roman Catholicism forced upon them by the sword and remain Catholic to this day. North America (with the exception of Quebec and Louisiana) was spared the dominance of Roman Catholicism because it was settled largely by Protestants.
Nor have the descendants of Aztecs, Incas, and Mayas forgotten that Roman Catholic priests, backed by the secular sword, gave their ancestors the choice of conversion (which often meant slavery) or death. They made such an outcry when John Paul II in a recent visit to Latin America proposed elevating Junipero Serra (a major eighteenth-century enforcer of Catholicism among the

Indians) to sainthood that the pope was forced to hold the ceremony in secret."

An army of 200 guards the Vatican

The City with Seven Hills is also known as Babylon the Great

They will stand at a distance, terrified by her great torment. They will cry out, "How terrible, how terrible for you, O Babylon, you great city! In a single moment God's judgment came on you." – Revelation 18:10

When the Book of Revelation was written, another name for Rome was "Babylon." Saint Peter, in his first of three letters, writes:

Your sister church here in Babylon sends you greetings, and so does my son Mark. – 1 Peter 5:13

Peter is widely believed to have been writing from Rome.

St. Peter's Square in the Vatican

Even Catholic apologist Karl Keating, in his book *Catholicism and Fundamentalism: The Attack on "Romanism*, admits that Rome has long been known as Babylon. He writes:

"Babylon is a code word for Rome. It is used that way six times in the last book of the Bible [four of the six are in chapters 17 and 18..." Also, "Eusebius Pamphilius, writing about 303, noted that "it is said that Peter's first epistle...was composed at Rome itself; and that he himself indicates this, referring to the city figuratively as Babylon."

This cannot be a reference to ancient Babylon for it did not sit on seven hills.

There are several historical studies that support the identification of Rome as being "Babylon the great" – cf. Bauckham (1993); Collins (1980); Friesen (1993); Giesen (1996); Kraybill (1996); Biguzzi (1998).

The Blood of God's People is on Her Hands

Do to her as she has done to others. Double her penalty for all her evil deeds. She brewed a cup of terror for others, so brew twice as much for her. - Revelation 18:6

In your streets flowed the blood of the prophets and of God's holy people and the blood of people slaughtered all over the world. – Revelation 18:24

There have been several inquisitions of the Catholic Church. Collectively they can be called "The Inquisition." We will touch briefly on the three most prominent. The first was the Medieval Inquisition that began in southern France in 1184 and did not officially end until the 1960s. Quite separate was the infamous Spanish Inquisition that began in 1478 and ended in 1834. Then there was the Roman Inquisition that began in 1542 and continued until the mid-1800s. The various inquisitions spanned a period of about a millennium.

The Inquisitions were judicial tribunals made up mostly of Roman Catholic Church clergymen. Their charge was to locate, try and sentence people that the Church believed to be guilty of heresy.

The purpose of the inquisitions was to secure and maintain religious and doctrinal unity in the Roman Catholic Church and throughout the Holy Roman Empire through the conversion, torture or execution of alleged heretics.

In these Inquisitions, vast numbers of people were tortured and/or murdered by the Catholic Church. Some of those found to be "heretics" were women accused of being witches, Muslims, Knights Templar, critics of the Church and many non-Catholic Christians who would not give up their faith in salvation through Jesus Christ alone and swear their allegiance to the Catholic Church. They would not yield to her heresies or confess what they did not believe.

It will never be known how many persons died for their beliefs at the hands of the Catholic Church…burned at the stake, tortured to death, or simply left to die from malnutrition or sickness in cold, dank, dark prisons. Whether the number is in the hundreds of thousands, or the tens of millions as some speculate, we can be reasonably sure that the Catholic Church with its great power and wealth engaged the most talented people to rewrite history and sanitize historical records wherever possible.

Whatever the number of those killed, many times more people were tortured into submission. God saw it all and he does not forget!

The Santa Rota Romana, the judicial tribunal of the Catholic Church

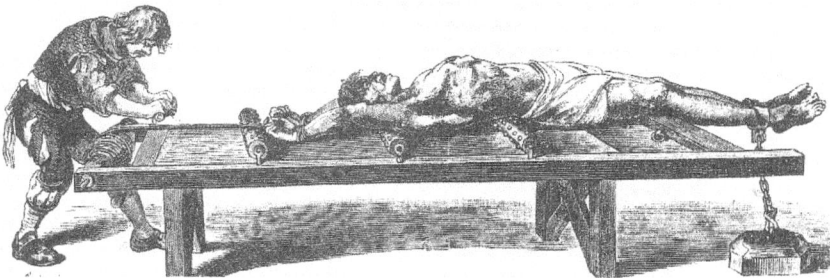

The **Medieval Inquisition** was due in part to the increasing moral corruption of the clergy in the Catholic Church. Sects rose up to challenge the Church's acceptance of bribes to approve otherwise illegal marriages, and the possession of extreme wealth by the clergy, among other things. The Inquisition's main focus was to eradicate these sects. Some inquisitors enriched themselves by confiscating property of the "heretics," others by the sale of absolutions. In 1252, Pope Innocent IV issued a papal bull authorizing the use of torture by inquisitors.

The brutal **Spanish Inquisition** primarily targeted Jews who professed to be of the Catholic faith but refused to give up certain Jewish religious practices. They were known as Crypto-Jews.

The **Roman Inquisition** was responsible for prosecuting individuals accused of a wide array of "crimes" related to heresy, sorcery, immorality, blasphemy and witchcraft. As with the Spanish Inquisition, Crypto-Jews were again a favorite target.

A woman being burned at the stake

Her Extravagances Have Made the Merchants of the World Rich

The Woman wore purple and scarlet clothing and beautiful jewelry made of gold and precious gems and pearls. In her hand she held a gold goblet... - Revelation 17:4

Because of her desires for extravagant luxury, the merchants of the world have grown rich. - Revelation 18:3

The merchants of the world will weep and mourn for her, for there is no one left to buy their goods. She bought great quantities of gold, silver, jewels, and pearls; fine linen, purple, silk, and scarlet cloth; things made of fragrant thyine wood, ivory goods, and objects made of expensive wood; and bronze, iron, and marble. She also bought cinnamon, spice, incense, myrrh, frankincense, wine, olive oil, fine flour, wheat, cattle, sheep, horses, chariots, and bodies – that is, human slaves. - Revelation 18:11-13

Following are excerpts from *The Vatican Billions* by Avro Manhattan, published in 1983 (italics):

"The Vatican's treasure of solid gold has been estimated by the United Nations World Magazine to amount to several billion dollars. A large bulk of this is stored in gold ingots with the U.S. Federal Reserve Bank, while banks in England and Switzerland hold the rest. But this is just a small portion of the wealth of the

Vatican, which in the U.S. alone, is greater than that of the five wealthiest giant corporations of the country. When to that is added all the real estate, property, stocks and shares abroad, then the staggering accumulation of the wealth of the Catholic Church becomes so formidable as to defy any rational assessment."

"The Catholic Church is the biggest financial power, wealth accumulator and property owner in existence. She is a greater possessor of material riches than any other single institution, corporation, bank, giant trust, government or state on the whole globe."

There is no reasonable way of assessing the actual financial condition of the Roman Catholic Church. Its finances are exceptionally complex spanning many countries. There are more bank accounts than any one person knows of. The value of her real estate holdings throughout the world, including cathedrals, basilicas and churches defies calculation. There are approximately 3,200 cathedrals and 2,200 basilicas in addition to parish and abbey churches.

If you have had the opportunity to tour some of the magnificent Catholic cathedrals around the world, you were probably amazed by their grandeur and opulence, the beautiful imported marbles, tapestries and costly gold adornments. The Vatican museum holds a vast collection of priceless artwork, sculptures and jewels.

Rituals, pageantry and costly clerical vestments

Consider the following description of the coronation of Pope Gregory IX (1227-1241):

"On the day of his coronation he proceeded to St. Peter's, accompanied by several prelates, and assumed the pallium according to custom; and after having said mass he marched to the palace of the Lateran, covered with gold and jewels. On Monday, having said mass at St. Peter's, he returned wearing two crowns, mounted on a horse richly caparisoned, and surrounded by Cardinals clothed in purple, and a numerous clergy. The streets were spread with tapestry, inlaid with gold and silver, the noblest productions of Egypt, and the most brilliant colors of India, and perfumed with various aromatic odors" (George Waddington, A History of the Church from the Earliest Ages to the Reformation, 1834, p. 335).

Music and the Happy Voices of Brides and Grooms Will Never Be Heard in Her Again

The sound of harps, singers, flutes, and trumpets will never be heard in you again. No craftsmen and no trades will ever be found in you again. The sound of the mill will never be heard in you again. 23The light of a lamp will never shine in you again. The happy voices of brides and grooms will never be heard in you again. For your merchants were the greatest in the world, and you deceived the nations with your sorceries. – Revelation 18:22-23

Chapter 8

God Has Decreed her Destruction

A Sudden, Violent Event

The Great Prostitute will be destroyed for leading souls astray, for killing God's saints, and bringing shame upon his Holy Name!

> *She glorified herself and lived in luxury, so match it now with torment and sorrow. She boasted in her heart, "I am queen on my throne. I am no helpless widow, and I have no reason to mourn." Therefore these plagues will overtake her in a single day - death and mourning and famine. She will be completely consumed by fire, for the Lord God who judges her is mighty. – Revelation 18:7-8*

The Bible speaks of a sudden, violent event, or events, that will destroy the Great Prostitute. That could mean the destruction of Vatican City or the entire City of Rome with the subsequent death of the whole church. Or it could mean something more cataclysmic. Ominously, whatever God has in store for the Church, he wants his people to come out of her so they will not share in her punishment. I don't know what that means, but I would take it very seriously!

The scarlet beast and his ten horns all hate the prostitute. They will strip her naked, eat her flesh, and burn her remains with fire. For God has put a plan into their minds, a plan that will carry out his purposes. – Revelation 17:16-17

And the kings of the world who committed adultery with her and enjoyed her great luxury will mourn for her as they see the smoke rising from her charred remains. They will stand at a distance, terrified by her great torment. Revelation 18:9-10

The merchants who became wealthy by selling her these things will stand at a distance, terrified by her great torment. They will weep and cry out, "How terrible, how terrible for that great city! She was clothed in finest purple and scarlet linens, decked out with gold and precious stones and pearls! In a single moment all the wealth of the city is gone!" – Revelation 18:15-17

And all the captains of the merchant ships and their passengers and sailors and crews will stand at a distance. They will cry out as they watch the smoke ascend, and they will say, "Where is there another city as great as this?" And they will weep and throw dust on their heads to show their grief. And they will cry out, "How terrible, how terrible for that great city! The shipowners became wealthy by transporting her great wealth on the seas. In a single moment it is all gone." - Revelation 18:17-19

Rejoice over her fate, O heaven and people of God and apostles and prophets! For at last God has judged her for your sakes. – Revelation 18:20

Then a mighty angel picked up a boulder the size of a huge millstone. He threw it into the ocean and shouted, "Just like this, the great city Babylon will be thrown down with violence and will never be found again. Revelation 18:21

An aerial view of the Vatican, the smallest country in the world

The Bible says people will stand in disbelief at her smoking ruins, possibly much like we all sat in disbelief in front of our televisions watching the Twin Towers collapse on September 11, 2001

A Celebration in Heaven

After this, I heard what sounded like a vast crowd in heaven shouting, "Praise the Lord! Salvation and glory and power belong to our God. His judgments are true and just. He has punished the great prostitute who corrupted the earth with her immorality. He has avenged the murder of his servants." And again their voices rang out: "Praise the Lord! The smoke from that city ascends forever and ever!" – Revelation 19:1-3

May God richly bless you as you grow in your knowledge of him and his will for your life. God tells us that if we seek him with all our heart, we will find him…along with the peace, joy and eternal life he brings with him. If you would be interested in joining a Bible study group, one I've heard many good things about is Bible Study Fellowship, also known as BSF. To inquire about classes in your area, go to www.bsfinternational.org – Ken March

www.ingramcontent.com/pod-product-compliance
Lightning Source LLC
Chambersburg PA
CBHW061748020426
42331CB00006B/1391